JANETTA HARVEY lives with he
their three dogs. They divide th
and south-west France. Janetta
campaigner against puppy far
commercially-driven puppy bree
Saving Susie-Belle.

Also by Janetta Harvey

Saving Susie-Belle

Saving
One More

JANETTA HARVEY

SilverWood

Published in 2015 by SilverWood Books

SilverWood Books Ltd
14 Small Street, Bristol, BS1 1DE, United Kingdom
www.silverwoodbooks.co.uk

ISBN 978-1-78132-398-4 (paperback)
ISBN 978-1-78132-399-1 (ebook)

British Library Cataloguing in Publication Data
A CIP catalogue record for this book is available from
the British Library

Set in Sabon by SilverWood Books
Printed by Berforts Information Press on responsibly sourced paper

To all those whose stories never get told

Don't walk in front of me; I may not follow.
Don't walk behind me; I may not lead.
Just walk beside me and be my friend.
                                    – Albert Camus

Foreword

With so much animal cruelty happening around the world, it is easy to think that it is just something that occurs elsewhere, in other countries, not the UK. After all, dolphin slaughter, bear bile farming, big game trophy hunting, bullfighting – none of these acts of cruelty happen on our doorstep.

But, while social media channels are flooded with images and horrific footage of faraway, 'exotic' cruelty, there is an animal welfare catastrophe happening right here in the UK that many people are still unaware of: puppy farming. This is an industry involving commercial businesses breeding puppies for profit with little or no regard for the welfare of not just the puppies, but of their parents too. There are hundreds of these places around the UK, where dogs are kept in small, cramped, filthy pens their whole lives without sufficient veterinary care, food, water, treats, toys, exercise, basic grooming, or normal social interaction with other dogs or humans. To further increase profits, a typical breeding bitch on a puppy farm is bred as often as possible, which can be twice a year, without rest between litters, her pitiful life lasting only for as long as her body manages to hold out. It is an industry that makes people a lot of money but at a terrible cost to its victims, the dogs.

As a practising vet and animal welfare campaigner I meet and treat sick puppies all the time. Many are sourced responsibly, either from ethical breeders or reputable rescue organisations, but sadly the majority are bought on impulse, perhaps as a gift, found and ordered online to be delivered the next day, or spotted in a pet shop or with a local private dealer. They have come from puppy farms, or back street breeding places. I have been campaigning to tackle puppy farming and the sale of puppies in pet shops and other retail and online outlets for years. A few years ago I set up a non-profit organisation called Pup Aid, directly as a result of treating an influx of puppies born on puppy farms – all dying of parvovirus – in my vet clinic. I am deeply disturbed by the physical and psychological damage inflicted on dogs, by an industry that exists not only in the UK but in many countries around the world.

Giving birth to litter after litter with minimal or no medical care takes a terrible toll, with a typical breeding bitch on a puppy farm eventually dying, perhaps without having ventured more than a few feet from the spot where she was born. As a 'canine breeding machine' she will remain unnamed, unloved, her entire life. She may also live forever in constant fear, broken only by the love that she lavishes on her babies until they are taken away from her – often far too early and not properly weaned. Maybe she will be one of the very few that are 'retired' and taken into rescue; if not she will become just another nameless statistic, destroyed when she is no longer productive.

Puppies born into these inhumane conditions unsur-prisingly lack sufficient immune system development, and are often burdened with infection and parasites; they miss out on important socialisation. These underage pups then face a tortuous journey, typically crammed into vehicles with batches of other pups, travelling hundreds of miles without their mothers, to be delivered to pet shops, garden centres, or other retail outlets; or sold by dealers acting as breed-ers from homes around the country. Increased stress levels during this horrific experience result in frequent defecation and urination, maximizing the risk of spreading infectious diseases such as parvovirus and kennel cough.

With trauma like this, coupled with the stress they experience during transit when they are shipped to the points of sale, it is no wonder the practices followed by puppy farms are responsible for so many of the dogs produced by them suffering health and behavioural problems. Sick puppies sold in shops, which many people are shocked are still legal outlets for selling puppies, seem more likely to die shortly after purchase. They frequently incubate deadly infections (a likely reason for their lethargy in the pet shop environment), which then develop into full blown disease after arriving in their new home. In my professional experience I have seen puppies succumb to parvovirus just hours after purchase. All this results in high emotional and financial costs for new owners.

This animal abuse is happening on our doorstep 24/7 – and what is worse, most of this activity is totally legal, permitted by ineffective, outdated, and poorly enforced legislation. So we need to work out a way of effectively tackling this situation; to stop puppy farming and all its associated inhumanities towards those who simply cannot protect themselves. Positive change is urgently needed.

Where Janetta Harvey's first book, *Saving Susie-Belle*, focussed closely on the UK situation and her experience as an adopter of Susie-Belle, just one of the millions of victims of puppy farming, this book goes farther, exploring just how damaging the industry is across the world. It is disgraceful that puppy farming, an industry run on lines akin to livestock production, is allowed to flourish in any country that considers dogs as companions; beloved pets that live with us in our homes.

People need to know what they might be supporting when they source puppies today. This book is an important one, for Janetta Harvey exposes the truth that lies behind the cute puppies being bought in their millions around the world. Janetta shines a light on a global industry that exploits companion animals simply so that money can be made.

Through telling the stories of her own dogs and others who have existed and just about survived in the puppy farming business – the struggle they have to live normal lives once they are rescued – Janetta brings it home just how dreadful the reality is for the dogs caught up in it.

But there is hope and humour in this book: Janetta and her husband Michel show that while the many years their dogs suffered have taken their toll, the amazing capacity that dogs show to forgive and move on with their new lives, given a chance, is intact, even in dogs that have never lived with humans, and have known only cruelty until their rescue. But, they should not have had to endure what victims of puppy farming have to. The current massive demand and subsequent supply of cheaply produced puppies will end, in part, by educating the puppy-buying public. This book is a great contribution to that. Read on, and tell others, and one day soon there will be no more dogs like Susie-Belle or Twinkle to save.

– Marc Abraham BVM&S MRCVS
Winner of Vet of the Year
CEVA Animal Welfare Awards 2014

Preface

The first book I wrote about puppy farming, *Saving Susie-Belle*, is a personal account of life shared with our dog, Susie-Belle, a survivor of the brutal puppy farming industry. The book covers our first year with her, as my husband Michel and our other dog, Renae, helped her to live as a normal dog for the first time in her life. She arrived in our home traumatised, damaged both physically and psychologically and knowing nothing about living with humans. Her whole life had been limited to a few square feet of concrete in the back of a filthy, dark, disused agricultural barn. She had been nothing more than a breeding machine, in an endless cycle of producing puppies in an industry that values dogs only for their fertility. It is a business that nearly killed Susie-Belle, but thankfully she was fortunate to survive long enough to get out, and get a chance at life. Most never do.

Before she came into our life I knew a little about puppy farming, but after living with her for just a short while, seeing the damage done to Susie-Belle, I discovered things about how dogs are treated by those in the industry which I could not have imagined. I wrote *Saving Susie-Belle* both as a personal account of our life together, but also to highlight the cruelty that exists in the brutal, commercial world of puppy breeding that she survived. But since writing that book, I have learnt much more, and had stories shared with me of many, many dogs whose blighted lives are a damning demonstration of just how brutally shameful the modern puppy breeding business can be. Millions of puppies are bred and sold each year around the world, and a large proportion of them leave parents behind in places similar to that where Susie-Belle suffered for years.

I hoped by writing *Saving Susie-Belle* it would be my contribution to raising awareness in people's minds about what is going on behind the deluge of images of cute puppies we see all the time. I believed that this, plus saving one dog and helping her to enjoy life, would bring a sense of peaceful satisfaction that I had done something useful in the world; that I might have made a difference, however tiny. I thought that by reading the book, it might make a bit of an impact on some as to where they source their dogs from. That it might stop even one sale of a puppy-farmed puppy going ahead. That by enjoying the book and sharing Susie-Belle's adventures, it would make people think about adopting from rescue and saving a life like hers. By seeing how she now enjoys days of peace and days of small adventures it would bring home the awful reality of what she had to endure to get to where she now is, and readers would want this to end for all dogs. From contact with readers around the world, I know this has happened, and this is pleasing; it lets me feel the work of writing the book was worthwhile, that Susie-Belle's life is changing things for other dogs.

However, I have no sense of peace, no feeling of a job completed, for I am gripped by a fiery, consuming, passionate belief that I have to do more. That writing one book, saving one dog and sharing her story, is not enough. It is nowhere close to being sufficient when I see daily the massive scale of misery being inflicted on dogs. There is so much that needs to be done. I know I cannot save them all, or even many, but I can and must do more to change things for the better – as can everyone. In fact every person who cares about dogs should be doing something, and this is what *Saving One More* hopes to inspire. Here, I look farther afield than in the first book.

One striking thing that publishing *Saving Susie-Belle* brought about for me was an awareness of the global nature of the suffering that Susie-Belle experienced. I have been contacted by people around the world who are battling to make a difference, to end the suffering in the puppy breeding industry. They want to change things, and in the following pages I share some of the stories of dogs, campaigners and rescuers, with the dual aim of paying tribute to them and inspiring others to follow. Where requested, names and identities are changed in order to protect their privacy or in some cases any future rescue work.

There are many inspirational people and dogs whose stories you will find within these pages and I hope, like me, you are fired up to get involved, and to share with others what you read, enjoy and at times get deeply frustrated by. It is a mystery to me how a lot of what goes on in the UK and elsewhere is entirely legal, despite being wholly unacceptable to those of us who care, with our hearts and minds, about dogs.

Readers of *Saving Susie-Belle* may detect an occasional angrier, more frustrated emotional thread weaving through the book, for that is how I feel. I know so much now that I was ignorant to when Susie-Belle began her journey with us, and it makes me cross. I boil with rage at times, if I allow myself to dwell on the knowledge that the people who caused her suffering will most likely be doing the exact same thing today to Susie-Belle's replacement, for I have little doubt they are still in business. Nothing is yet stopping the misery for dogs like her. And I feel sad and need readers to feel the same so it will one day be over and a better world for the dogs will arrive. But it is some way off just yet. Some days it seems farther than others. I hope to lead readers on a journey that will bring it closer as it is only by us all doing our bit, collectively and individually, wherever in the world we are, that real improvements will come about.

The anger I feel, however, is always tempered by a glance

at the peaceful face of Susie-Belle, sitting beside me, for she is here to teach me many lessons, of that I am certain. While anger is justified, its bedfellow bitterness is destructive, it hinders progress, and I have learnt from Susie-Belle that more is achieved by positivity and moving onward than hanging onto negative thoughts and emotions. In the words of the American poet Ralph Waldo Emerson,

> For every minute you are angry you lose sixty seconds of happiness.

So, while a certain anger lies within these pages, there is also a healthy sprinkling of hope and happiness, for without these I could slip into being little more useful than a raving mad dog-woman. The world probably doesn't need another one of those as they get too easily dismissed as just that, raving mad, and the big bad world of puppy farming continues unabated, by ignoring the crazies ranting and shouting from the sidelines. No, I know what is needed is engagement in the process and this I hope the book will encourage in others. Stewing on how frustrating I find the ongoing injustices for dogs is not my way, as it clogs my thoughts and drags me down to a depressing place where I have no wish to spend time. In any case, being in a perpetual state of angry frustration is too exhausting when I want our dogs to enjoy the fullest lives possible. Lives which you'll read here are divided between the busy urban south of England and the peace of rural France where we spend a lot of our time, walking the trails of the countryside, wild swimming, and all in all ensuring life for our dogs is as perfect as we can make it. All this helps to keep the darker moments in check, when the big picture, the shocking global scale of puppy breeding problems is examined.

What in the UK and Australia are called puppy farms, in the United States and Canada are known as puppy mills. Other terms used include factory farms, puppy factories and battery farms. All describe the same thing: commercial breeding facilities where dogs are confined to breed with profit being first and foremost, and usually the only desired outcome. The welfare of the breeding parents and puppies is given scant, if any, attention. Different countries have their own regulatory systems, standards and licensing requirements but what is common to all countries is inadequate enforcement, and standards that fall far short of what welfare campaigners consider acceptable, let alone optimum.

For ease of reading, throughout the book I tend to stick with the term puppy farming to describe commercial breeding that is primarily done for money; the type of activity that leads to millions of dogs leading lives that they have not evolved to live. But, I include within the term dogs kept in smaller scale, breeding facilities that confine dogs for the majority of their time, and offer a minimum of care, even if these places meet licensing and regulatory requirements in their respective countries. I also include what are sometimes referred to as backstreet or backyard breeders, those who breed indiscriminately and purely for the money they can make from the dogs. I use the terms 'industry' or 'business' to refer to all these breeders. Anyone who puts two dogs together and a litter results is a breeder; they may also happen to be a puppy farmer.

As puppy buyers, we have the choice and moral obligation to go to ethical breeders – and I know they exist – or to consider adoption. Anything less contributes to animal abuse, although many puppy buyers would understandably balk at that accusation. I exclude from my ire breeders who place monetary gain way down on their list of reasons to breed; those who breed because they wish to protect their chosen breed, they do it right, they health test appropriately, they do not cut corners and they take responsibility for the lives they bring into the world. They show genuine love for all the dogs in their lives, they do not keep them separate from the home, their dogs live as dogs should live – with their human companions, not apart. These breeders exist but they are far outnumbered by others who do it badly and for reasons I find abhorrent.

It may be called different things in different places, but the force which drives the industry is the same: money. Dogs are seen as nothing more than a cash crop. The money that is made from selling puppies around the world is huge. It is a big, international business, the scale and detail of which is depressing to anyone who cares about the health, welfare and lives of dogs. Susie-Belle may have lived the majority of her life in a miserable puppy farm in the UK, but millions of other Susie-Belles are enduring the same, whether in the heat of an Australian puppy factory, or the frigid, freezing winter of an Iowan puppy mill, or the filth of an Eastern European puppy farm. Dogs trapped and suffering, so that money can be made from the thriving trade in their puppies. And it is a thriving, shameful, modern business. One that would not exist without the millions of puppy buyers keeping the trade buoyant. It is the buyers that are making the market the lucrative place it is right now. Without their demands the unscrupulous breeders would not be selling. The market would be a tough place to function in and they would find easier ways to make money.

Educating those who are providing the market for the puppies that dogs like Susie-Belle are forced to produce is one way to tackle the trade in misery and this is what this book hopes to do. It takes up where *Saving Susie-Belle* ended, only Susie-Belle and Renae are joined by a new sister, Twinkle. We have saved one more. Twinkle's story runs throughout the book; she has the same background as Susie-Belle but a different scale of damage and challenge. Where Susie-Belle taught me the supreme importance of endless patience, Twinkle's lessons are harder to fathom and a lot less obvious. Patience clearly, but there is more she is here to teach me. Nothing at all is straightforward with her. Nothing. She is a smart dog, but spends a lot of the time bewildered, although this gets less each week. She makes us smile each and every day, but often for reasons those new to puppy farm dogs might find cause to weep, not smile, over. The first time it took ten minutes for her to feel calm enough to have her lead put on, I grinned, as this was better than the twenty she had needed up to then. If I misread her signs of readiness for being picked up and she farts rather than poops in terror as I lift her, this is progress and makes me smile. I probably find a Twinkle fart a little more mirth-making than I really should. So much more significance gets attached to Twinkle's wind than the average dog, but nothing about her, not even her gas, is average.

What were once whispers of animal activism in my head, got louder as Susie-Belle crept along her tortuous path to recovery, becoming a shrill call when I saw what damage Twinkle lives with and how hard she has to work just to allow herself to feel even the briefest moment of happiness. In sharing Twinkle's tribulations, as well as the funny side of life with our marvellous, muddled up girl, I'm rather hoping enough people will fall in love with her, as they have sweet Susie-Belle, that they will join the fight to end the industry that has made her time on earth so hard. Now Twinkle has the chance to be happy and each day we spend together, she instils in me a dedication to make things better.

As my journey into this topic continues, the lines I draw as to what I find acceptable are drawn firmer; what may have been blurry grey areas to me at one stage are now crisp and clear. I no longer stay quiet or neutral where I once would have. I take inspiration from the words of the Nobel Peace prizewinning humanitarian writer, Elie Wiesel:

Neutrality helps the oppressor, never the victim. Silence encourages the tormentor, never the tormented.
                                                        – *The Night Trilogy*

I hope readers find enough inspiration in these pages to do what they can to end the suffering of breeding dogs around the world. To speak up; not to be indifferent to what they see, hear, read and know. I want to persuade people who care, even if that is just a tiny bit of caring, or a conscience tweaked, to do something. It is only by speaking up, by acting, by raising our collective voice across the globe that it will change. Together we can do this. In writing this book, I have taken Eleanor Roosevelt's advice and hope others will follow:

> Do what you feel in your heart to be right, for you'll be criticised anyway.

1

Susie-Belle is Saved

When we demean and exploit animals, we do no less to ourselves.

— Dr Michael Fox, veterinarian

When Susie-Belle joined our family in August 2011 she could have had no idea of the impact her life would have on us. But then neither could we. We had adopted her knowing full well that being a survivor of the puppy farming business would bring more than the average set of issues rescuing a dog might entail. We were prepared and happy for our lives to change in order to give her the life she deserved and had waited so many years for. However, what I did not realise was the complete takeover of mine that would follow. Once the full, horrific extent of the damage inflicted on Susie-Belle by those who had profited from her was really understood, I knew that I could not turn away from the millions of others still trapped. Seeing Susie-Belle recover from years of trauma and blossom into a true, in all possible ways, beautiful dog, starkly brought home to me that most dogs from her background will never have that chance. My eyes were already open when Susie-Belle came to us, and she has made sure they don't close on the ongoing tragedy for dogs that puppy farming is around the world.

Susie-Belle's first year or so living in our family taught us many things about what it is like to take a dog that has lived her entire life cooped up in a cruel environment, devoid of caring human contact, and to place her into an alien world – a world that for most dogs should be far from alien, for they have been living companionably among humans for many thousands of years. But through Susie-Belle and others, Michel and I saw first-hand that for dogs who are unfortunate enough to find themselves caught up in the puppy breeding industry, their existence is so far removed from what they are supposed to be, it can take a long time to overcome what the industry inflicts upon them. They are not companions but are part of a global business that makes vast sums of money for those who breed, sell and deal in their puppies. They are at best seen as livestock, a state of existence that dogs have never before been condemned to on anything like the scale seen now, if at all; at worst they are machines for making money that are given merely the basics to keep their hearts beating and their wombs and bodies productive.

Susie-Belle had lived and survived in that world for several years and for her, like the few who survive long enough to eventually find their way through rescuers into the homes of normal, caring humans, it was a bewildering experience to be given a chance at life. For these traumatised dogs have to learn everything about what it means to live among humans. Not humans who are indifferent to their needs, but people who actively seek them out and choose to care for them, shower them in love, hug and cuddle them despite this being most likely terrifying for the dogs. All this is normal, human-to-dog behaviour in an average household, but it must seem utterly confusing and frightening to an animal that has known only cruelty from mankind. In her years of confinement, Susie-Belle had endured a depth of abuse and harm that in our darker moments, Michel and I doubted she could ever properly recover from. But bit by bit, as we settled into sharing our lives with Susie-Belle, not only did she learn how to live a normal life in our home, we came to learn what she truly needed. Together we muddled along, doing our best, winging a lot of it, hoping to avoid too many mistakes as we went. As we tuned into a shared wavelength, we picked up more of what she required and subtly adapted our ways to help her to heal.

Three key things stand out in my mind as being essential in the process: us maintaining a quiet, gentle manner at all times, having an abundance of patience and keeping good daily routines. All this allowed Susie-Belle to know what to expect and removed a lot of her worries about what might be happening next in her scary new world. As she got to grips with living with us, we got used to adapting our ways too. We never rushed or forced her to do anything and remained vigilant for signs of stress. But being patient was not enough – necessary, but not enough – and we took up opportunities to nudge her along with new challenges, each one helping her to experience life as fully as she now deserved. We were determined not to smother her, not to keep her entirely out of the noisy, chaotic world around us. We committed to teaching her how to trust that new experiences were good things for her, and that we would always keep her safe. We shared mini adventures with Susie-Belle to help her develop; we took her walking on blustery beaches for the first time in her life, or into the city, and enjoyed regular days out with human and canine friends. As each successful day ended, we knew that she had crept a little farther along the road to being a happy dog.

It took me a while to recognise properly that all this could only be done at her pace – there could be no rush to help her enjoy life, however much I wanted to propel her on to happiness. We may have made a few errors in judging exactly what she could manage, but overall we got it about right in her first year or so. In some cases it can take months for dogs with Susie-Belle's background to adapt to living in homes, but years is more typical before it can really be said they are living normal lives. For some, the trauma can be too great to ever fully overcome and they remain permanently damaged.

Thankfully in Susie-Belle's case, as we journeyed along together and the months passed we knew that she could heal. We provided the time, care and love – plenty of each – that she needed in order to be physically and mentally healthy and she did the rest. Bit by bit Susie-Belle let herself trust us. Just a few shoots of confidence appeared to start with; not a lot, but enough in the beginning to help convince her, and us, that together we were on the right path. Over the months, those nascent signs of recovery strengthened, and we saw a gentle blossoming of Susie-Belle's true, adorable nature. By the end of her first year with us, she was well on the way to living happily.

She experienced many things for the first time in her life during that year. We took up camping as people told us dogs love it, and in her case this was true as she embraced it with obvious pleasure. She accompanied me on many swims in rivers and lakes and proved to be a natural swimmer, relaxed in the water – unlike her canine sister Renae who hates the very idea. We also ventured out on numerous organised walks across the country, offering her the chance to socialise with a diverse range of people and dogs; this built her confidence and gave her new, solidly pleasant memories to drown out the bad. At least that was our hope. We attended fun dog shows and she won top place as Dog of Courage at her first one; she travelled regularly to our second home in France where we spend time throughout the year and she came with us to a handful of tourist attractions both in the UK and there. Getting Susie-Belle out and about and savouring life filled our days, weeks and months as we relished seeing her confidence grow and her anxieties subside.

In our home food is a great joy, and as Michel is a professional chef, providing excellent meals and tasty pleasures for all under his roof, for the first time in her life Susie-Belle enjoyed delicious meals. She showed herself to be a genuine canine gourmet, relishing every meal and new taste experience. Giving her wholesome, home prepared meals not only provided enjoyment, it nourished her weakened body and helped her to be healthy. It is reasonable to assume that she had lived her entire life, from the moment she took her first breath, in the puppy farm that became her prison for so many years, and that life of deprivation and malnourishment would never have led to her being healthy. Her health began in our home with us, of that we are certain. Puppies born to poorly mothers struggle to thrive but most will leave their mothers and be sold into the pet market; others remain behind, to begin their breeding lives at the earliest age possible. Undoubtedly this was Susie-Belle's life before us and one that in her first year with us we did everything to help her forget.

If we thought after a year she was happier than she had ever been before, after eighteen months we knew she was a completely different dog to the fragile, subdued one who had arrived in our world in August 2011. No longer did we need to search for signs of contentment, it was beyond any doubt that she now enjoyed her life. Indeed, she not only did so, but remarkably she had learnt to communicate that happiness to us in ways it was once unimaginable she would. She engaged with us from the moment we woke and with her sister Renae, would be bopping around, cajoling us to get moving with breakfast and a walk. She held eye contact confidently, which was once unheard of, and spoke with her beautiful, expressive eyes more than any dog I have ever come across. Now I know that when she is happy her eyes sparkle with a luminosity that is unmistakably powered by pure joy; when worried, this dims, her eyes narrow and I see we need to pay attention to what is bothering her. Susie-Belle's eyes reflect her mood and thoughts and in that first year she found a way, with me in particular, to communicate her inner self and needs through them. When I came across this quote from author, A. D. Williams, I truly understood its meaning:

Eyes do more than see. They also speak.

25

She had transformed from a dog that lay tucked up on her bed wishing not to be noticed, to one excitedly greeting Michel and I every time one of us returned home. Previously she hadn't moved, or had done so reluctantly. To see her once tight and rigid body bouncing through the house towards me, radiating joy, made me giggle every single time, and I returned her open, warm greeting with matching enthusiasm, without fail. The pleasure of this has not dimmed through passing time and familiarity; we still enjoy our Susie-Belle greetings, cherishing every single one. She continues to grow more animated, confident and cheeky, and we love her ever deeper.

As our first year came and went, when out on walks with other dogs she was soon the one pushing her way to the front of any queue when treats were dished out. Only the faintest, ghostliest trace of her earlier timidity and wariness of humans remained. She relished the routines of her life with us, sitting confidently and quickly at our feet at the first hint of dinner preparations; looking up into our eyes, hers like polished precious black onyx, bright and alert as if commanding us to see what a brilliant sit she was performing. Over time, with Renae as her lead, she had naturally picked up that by sitting at our feet she would be given something nice. In fact she would be given nice things pretty often just for being near us. We never expected her to sit to command in her first year for it seemed ridiculously unfair to make a dog who had never had anything good in her life conform to an artificially imposed behaviour for a tiny reward. She was not a dog who needed the structured discipline of such rituals; her needs were special and our boundaries were as broad as she wanted to push them. She had worked out how to manipulate the new species of human she lived with, as she became the companion dog she should always have been. Gratitude welled deep within me whenever she nudged a little farther into the world of living naturally, freely, with us.

Although much progress was underway with Susie-

Belle's emotional healing, it wasn't all good and there were still issues of anxiety in some situations that she carried with her. Maybe she always will. It was most notable in unfamiliar or noisy environments, particularly if no other dogs were close by from whom she could draw reassurance. But we kept our lives steady and focused on keeping her safe in any sticky situations and each week that passed the flashes of anxiety seemed less frequent and certainly not crippling as they had once been. When she was with us, in her safe, secure world, she was a relatively normal, contented dog.

Once Susie-Belle had been with us for eighteen months and she was settled, happy and healthy, it seemed a good time for us to think about finding her and Renae another friend to share their lives with.

2

Adding One More

Adopt the pace of nature: her secret is patience.
– Ralph Waldo Emerson

I had once thought that having two dogs would be enough canine company for us, but sharing Susie-Belle's presence and journey stirred something within me that I had not known existed: I wanted to offer our home to many dogs in need, loving them to the end of their days, giving them the care and compassion they'd never had. For practical reasons, all the while we travel to France every few weeks, it will have a limiting effect on how many dogs we can adopt, but once Susie-Belle was content, I knew we could add at least one more to our canine family. Michel was happy with Renae and Susie-Belle, but then, it has never been my ever patient, accommodating husband who has brought any animals into our home; he just gets on with accepting and loving them when they arrive.

When we first married and he was at work on a Saturday morning, it was me that went along to the local cat shelter, Katz Castle, and brought home a feisty, independent, grumpy tortoiseshell I named Peachie Popple who lived with us for fourteen years, only slightly mellowing in her old age. Michel soon saw my unilateral decision was good and was as happy living with a cat as he had been cat-free. Little ruffled his world in any case, as it was me who largely took care of her, with his backing when needed or desired. Cradled lovingly in his arms was where she peacefully died when the time came. Having never lived with a cat before, I thought all cats loathed being picked up and lashed out indiscriminately; I did not consider it odd that should I decide to brush her, I would need to do so wearing garden gloves to save my hands and arms from a vicious shredding. For me, my only experience was the great and characterful cat Peachie Popple, living up to every piece of the 'naughty tortie' stereotype I only much later discovered. If she decided to sink her teeth into my fingers to tell me she'd had enough stroking for now, wasn't that normal for cats? My friends were never enamoured by her feisty ways and failed to understand why Michel and I loved our bruiser of a cat. But we muddled along worshipping her for fourteen years, admiring her independent nature, loving even her irritability as that made her the cat she was, all the while accepting she probably did not love us back at all. She was my first pet-love and she taught me to respect her and her wishes and to do only as she wanted, just how she insisted it be done, and that was fair enough. We understood one another pretty quickly, and she did a good job of moulding me into shape for looking after those who over the years would follow her paw-steps to and through my heart.

When she died and I returned to Katz Castle to find my new feline friend, fate decided that the only cat that the shelter deemed suitable to come and live with us was another sparky, characterful tortoiseshell. Rosie had come from a neglectful home nine months previously, being dumped with six others outside the shelter gates late one night. She had been in a poor state and hated being handled, probably never having experienced this, or much kindness.

Being a long-haired Persian cat, the neglect caused her serious problems with her coat and skin and the shelter talked me through a catalogue of problems that they had dealt with during her time with them, all of which I would need to continue taking care of. This, coupled with being an irritable cat and obvious stress-head did not make her attractive to many visitors looking for a cat to join their family; she was overlooked time and time again. However, I was smitten the second I spotted her hiding at the back of the pen behind an old armchair, her huge owl-like eyes holding my gaze, sizing me up. It was a look I knew well (it had been a Peachie Popple classic) and home Rosie came to us.

Rosie lived initially with our first dog, Jasmine, then, when we lost her, with our lively puppy Renae and latterly Susie-Belle. During the time with Jasmine, Rosie had settled into being a calm, home-loving cat, with only hints of her former sparkiness. However, she never grew to accept being groomed and every day the same difficult task was performed, with the same outcome: for a few brief seconds she would put up with it, then decide that no, this was still an assault, an indignity she would not succumb to (albeit one always followed by a fishy treat). She would wriggle out of my hands, forcing me to abandon it once again, having brushed a miniscule amount of her extensive, long-haired coat. I persevered despite the daily trial, and through some miracle her coat always looked magnificent. In the eight years she spent with us, she became a seasoned traveller, coming with us to our house in France in her later years, sharing the journey with Jasmine, then Renae and Susie-Belle. When she died quite unexpectedly in 2013 I felt her loss keenly but knew she had at last known what it was to be peaceful and cherished, and allowed to live life on her terms.

With Susie-Belle settled and Rosie sadly gone from our lives, it was time to reach out to another animal in need of a home. In the search that resulted in Susie-Belle joining us and through writing her story and digging deeper into the dirty world of puppy farming, I have made a number of friends in animal rescue work. I have also come to understand more fully the dreadful extent of the problem the UK faces with unwanted dogs. To say it is sad is a ridiculous understatement, but greater words fail me when we see massive numbers of animals languishing in rescue, some for years awaiting adoption with many thousands being killed simply because there are not enough homes for them, or they are deemed too difficult to rehome. Yet, and here my bile rises, at the same time, the puppy business is booming. The trade in cuddly, sweet, adorable puppies grows ever stronger while the numbers of discarded, disposable dogs climbs.

There was no question that the dog who joined Susie-Belle and Renae would be from rescue, and having learnt what I now know about the lives and deaths of the majority of breeding dogs, she would be one from the terrible end of the breeding industry. It wasn't that I was particularly looking for a traumatised dog, and I was aware that despite great progress with Susie-Belle, her healing was ongoing and not something I would risk being distracted from or upsetting. No, it was the desperate suffering of dogs like her, hundreds of thousands of them in the UK alone, that I could not turn away from, which drew me to do something for at least one more. I knew that our home could and should include another damaged soul needing safe refuge for the remainder of their life. We have the resources and I felt a strong obligation to offer what I have available to another cruelly treated dog. Michel, although not as deeply immersed in this as I have dunked myself, felt much the same, without needing to know or absorb the details. He left it to me to get on with it. Wise man.

I was in no particular hurry to find our new friend, but as fate would have it, no sooner had the decision been made to add a third dog to our family than Janet, Susie-Belle's foster mum and manager of the Diana Brimblecombe Animal Rescue Centre (DBARC), took in Twinkle, a miniature schnauzer recently saved from the puppy farming industry. When I had first met Janet at the start of my quest to bring Susie-Belle into our family I could not have imagined how our friendship would develop and how committed I would become both to campaigning against puppy farming and supporting the work of DBARC. The day I first visited the centre, I had been ridiculously nervous. It seems faintly daft now how intense I felt about meeting Janet, little knowing we would become the firm friends we now are. Putting myself forward as a potential adopter and hoping I would pass muster was a new experience for me and one I took seriously. It is rare I ever do anything by halves once I decide on it and adopting Susie-Belle was a decision I had made. I just needed to persuade her highly professional, fiercely protective guardian of that.

Even at that early stage, I was smitten with Susie-Belle and in my heart she was already part of our family despite her not yet being healthy enough for adoption and me only seeing her on the Internet. But my sense of attachment to her was deeply intense and I was determined to be deemed good enough for her, so as I set off to meet her my nerves were high. This was all made worse by me getting lost in the Berkshire countryside and running late for our appointment. Being an irritating stickler for punctuality myself, I feared my tardiness would scupper any chance I had of being considered suitably responsible to adopt a dog. Thankfully it did not go against me, and since that day I've known how silly my anxieties were: there's a lot more to the judgement good rescues make about the suitability of adopters than their skills at map-reading and time-keeping. My own perception of what would make or break me as a candidate for Susie-Belle's adoption now seems naive and shallow as I've learnt more about the tough world of dog rescue, particularly of the poor survivors of the nasty world of puppy farming. If only it were so simple; that their problems could be magically wiped away by being taken home by someone who is punctual.

Janet and I share a frank, honest friendship and as I began to ponder adding to our canine family, I discussed with her on a few occasions the impact bringing another dog into our lives would have on Susie-Belle. I was acutely aware that when I get an idea in my head, my obsessive single-mindedness can, if not checked, squash the life out of annoying, competing thoughts that struggle to take hold in my mind, urging caution and contemplation. Rash actions have got me into all kinds of bother here and there my entire life, more so when I was younger and a lot more impulsive. These days, probably for the good, it falls to Michel to bring a contemplative halt to hectic, scattered ideas rushing through our household on a teeming surge of reckless enthusiasm. Frustrating as I can find this, it is usually a wise thing, with hindsight, to take the buzzing bee from my bonnet and instil some calm into the gathering swarm.

When I came to thinking about a third dog, although the bee stirred I had enough sense to know Janet should be sounded out before committing to anything. Caution for once kept the buzz to a gentle, unhurried hum as I thought the matter through. I was a little vague with Michel; I dropped a few hints, doing some practical planning, like getting a larger car and bigger dog beds, and I showed him a few online pictures of dogs looking for homes, all of which if he had wanted to, he could have spotted as signs a change was in the offing. I took his mild interest in the tales of this or that dog needing a home as tacit acceptance of the three-dog family I was preparing us for. It may not be everyone's idea of how these things should be done, but it is ours and has been the case for many years of happy marriage. Our 'not-to-be copied' recipe of me thinking, deciding, then doing it all in a mad rush, and Michel patiently living with, sharing and enjoying the consequences works. Mostly.

While I felt the rising of a strong urge to help another dog, I knew that I would never do anything that would jeopardise Susie-Belle's hard-earned happiness and trust. Once the seed was planted, before it sprouted into the obsession it was almost certainly likely to become, I knew I needed to chat over the issues with Janet, who understands them – and me. Having her as a confidante whom I knew I could debate truthfully with was a handy privilege; I understood that she would always put the interests of the dogs first even if this meant telling me things that I might not want to hear.

But in our chats I was relieved that she agreed there was no reason to think that bringing a third dog into our family should knock Susie-Belle from what was now her firm path of recovery. Janet was confident that Susie-Belle's progress was secure enough to enjoy having another dog, even one with difficulties, in the home. As far as Renae was concerned, I was certain that she would welcome a new addition, but as Susie-Belle's best friend I hoped the close companionship they shared would be enhanced, not upset as their canine group expanded. Although the doggy dynamics in the household would inevitably alter, I had faith that all involved would gain from the change.

Renae's confidence and friendly nature have been invaluable for Susie-Belle in helping her to learn how to live amongst humans. For puppy farming survivors this is a hard experience as their contact with humans is sparse, harsh and something to be feared. For a dog that has lived its entire life in a breeding environment, adapting to living in a normal household is greatly eased if there is a well adjusted, healthy resident dog to help them. We noticed early on with Susie-Belle that she took her cues from Renae and know that without her canine sister to lead the way, her journey to normality would have been considerably slower and less successful. For these reasons, most rescues that rehome breeding dogs insist on there being a resident dog, with occasional exceptions. Although dogs will do their best to adapt without the help of another one it will take longer and in some cases be less complete without having a good example to follow.

As Janet knew of my wish to adopt another dog, when Twinkle arrived with her there was little hesitation on either side to get a visit arranged, formalities processed, Twinkle recovering from her spay operation and heading home with us to start her new life. This was so different from the months of waiting that I had for Susie-Belle to be fit and well enough to join us, and it was just the first of many differences between our experiences with her and Twinkle.

3

Troubled Twinkle Arrives

Whenever a thing is done for the first time, it releases a little demon.

– Emily Dickinson

When Susie-Belle arrived with us, she had spent the previous six months living with Janet, learning what it was like for the first time ever to be cared for and loved. During that time she had met many of the basic challenges for a rescued puppy farm dog and was on her way to coping well with what is normal life for most dogs. Things like getting used to a collar or harness and lead are all new experiences for dogs that have been cooped up in a pen or cage for their entire lives and can be utterly terrifying. Anything around their necks in the past may well have been for harsh restraint. Susie-Belle was tied with rope around her neck in the place from where she was rescued. These dogs have to unlearn responses rooted deeply in trauma. A lot of things we take for granted with our pets hold nothing but grim memories for dogs brutalised by their past treatment, all of which take time – in some cases a lot of time – to fade.

House-training can be hard for them as they have only had their immediate environment in which to urinate and defecate. So contrary to a dog's natural preference not to soil their sleeping and living areas, for confined dogs this is overridden by their stark, cruel reality. It can mean when they start to live in homes where we understandably wish them to be clean, house-training can take an age to master. For some, they never fully manage to do so. Household noises such as washing machines, vacuum cleaners, doorbells and knockers – all these can be terrifying; not just the first time they are heard, but every time, for months, or even years after leaving the puppy farm behind.

Twinkle was just a month out of the misery when she came to us and brought with her issues related not only to the newness of her freedom, but to the particular damage the breeding business had inflicted on her. Where with Susie-Belle a lot of preparatory work and good foundations for life as a normal dog had been laid down with Janet, in Twinkle's case we were almost starting from scratch. Coupled with the different psychological problems she was burdened with, our early months were quite distinct from those with Susie-Belle. Twinkle has shown me first-hand that although there are similarities in the issues puppy farm dogs face once they are rescued, each one will be unique and have needs peculiar to them as the individuals that they are, and they deserve to be treated as such. It is wise to have no preconceived ideas about what behaviours and peculiarities a puppy farm survivor may bring. Twinkle, in her maddeningly confounding way, has shown me that in bucket loads.

I hoped that our experience with Susie-Belle would go a long way towards us nurturing and helping Twinkle without making too many mistakes as we went. Janet had warned me that the psychological issues she was battling were of a different order to Susie-Belle. Despite her having confidence that we would cope with whatever Twinkle came with to her new life, Janet needed to be sure that we were prepared for things with Twinkle to be complicated, at least in the early weeks. For example, she warned me that Twinkle might bite; if it happened it would arise only from fear, not aggression and she did not want me to lose confidence or be downhearted should it occur. I appreciated Janet mentioning it, but I wasn't worried; if it occurred, I knew it would be what Twinkle needed to do at the time and we would work through things together, whenever or however they happened. Not that I relished being bitten, but for Twinkle, I knew she had experienced a lot worse from humans and the ones she would now be spending the rest of her life with were not going to fail her, however hard or littered with painful nips the path ahead might become.

When we adopted Susie-Belle, I felt as prepared as I could be for someone with no experience of rehoming a dog, let alone one from her background. There was some anxiety about what her needs might be and how well she might settle, but that was far outweighed by all-consuming excitement about bringing her into our lives. Emotionally I was attached to her many weeks before she finally arrived in her new home with us. With Twinkle, while I was excited, I was a lot less impatient for her to start enjoying her life. I knew she would do it only when she was good and ready. Susie-Belle has taught me many things, and the need to be calm, patient and accepting at all times with our dogs tops the long list of life lessons she has imparted.

Although I always reminded myself in Susie-Belle's first year that she could only heal at her pace, not mine, however much help, encouragement – even at times gentle cajoling – I gave, it did take a long time for me to properly accept the reality. *Her* reality. Where in my head I repeated my mantra daily that 'time, time, time' would heal her, my heart pushed on ahead beyond where she actually was in her development. I wanted Susie-Belle to exorcise her demons quickly, to free herself and embrace fully the simple joy of living, much sooner than she was capable of. It is only with the passage of time and honest reflection that I know it took her much longer than I want to admit to be at ease in our home. Her first anniversary with us marked a clear turning point as we saw improvements increase and gather pace, a process that continues today. With this experience, at the beginning of Twinkle's time with us

I accepted at the outset that it might take a long while, possibly years, before the ghouls and ghastly nightmares that gripped her would ever leave her in peace to enjoy life.

Beyond the experience we had gained with Susie-Belle, my expectations for Twinkle were also shaped by hearing the numerous experiences of people with dogs from similar backgrounds that I have been privileged to get to know and in some cases be a part of. As my life has become more and more focused on campaigning against commercial and abusive puppy breeding, I have come to learn the great depth of injury to both body and mind that the factory farming of dogs is responsible for. I have immersed myself in a personal journey of understanding just how damaging the world of puppy production is to dogs' psychological functioning. My awareness continues to deepen as I find out more, and this has helped me to understand Twinkle's complex issues better. This has been essential for us as we have certainly needed to be confident with her in ways Susie-Belle never really required.

Where Susie-Belle's anxiety was, and to some extent still is, a quiet, persistent presence staying mostly in the shadows, Twinkle's anxiety is a big, brazen, nasty force that suddenly springs out, often without warning, startling both her and us. There is nothing subtle about the damaged psyche that Twinkle is burdened with. In the early days, her behaviour could best be described as unpredictable and skittish; one minute she would appear to be quite calmly sat in her bed, watching the household goings on, albeit with eyes wide open, scanning her surroundings, vigilant but quietly so. But, if I was tempted to approach with a desire to gently stroke an ear, or offer a tempting morsel to show her she was safe, welcome and loved – bang, out of her bed she would jump and fly off up the stairs, or out of the room, or down the garden if she could. Or if she was sharing the bed with Susie-Belle, as was often the case, she would suddenly leap up behind her sister, perching on the edge of the cushion, or on Susie-Belle's back, alarmed, alert, uneasy, eyes full of terror. Often a snoozing

Susie-Belle would be startled awake by Twinkle scrambling over her to get away from whoever was silly enough to assume she might like their caring attentions. She would even do this if no one had moved or glanced in her direction, but something had spooked her.

Although we didn't always know what had got her into a tizzy, we accepted that this was just our confused, changeable, adorable Twinkle for the time being and hoped it would improve for her soon enough. We knew it was how she needed to react and provided the time and space for her to work through things as we all adapted to living together. We soon learnt not to take for granted any signs we saw of her being at ease, for that might suddenly change with an out-of-the-blue ratcheting up of her stress, notch by frenzied notch. In the first few months, Twinkle could rapidly work her way into a bit of a stew that would take a disconcerting length of time – if judged by any commonplace standards – to dissipate. Upsetting as it was for us to see her react like this, we knew she would settle, and focused on the good moments and pushed aside fleeting concerns about how damaged she was. She would gain nothing by us fretting and worrying over the state she had been left in by the puppy farming industry; she was with us for the rest of her life; she was safe and we would help her. What she needed was our calm, loving assistance in finding herself, without us adding our own dramatics to her life.

In the first few days, she was terrified if we approached, cowering in the back of her crate that we left open so she could retreat into it whenever she felt the need – which was most of the time. So, we did not approach; we largely ignored her, leaving her to go in and out as she chose. She was extremely wary of us and easily panicked if we moved too quickly, or if she felt we were too close for comfort. Her years in the puppy farm had done this to her. Where she should naturally have felt joy from living as part of a calm and peaceful group, and sought comfort from being around us, her previous life of confinement with little human interaction had knocked this out of her. She had lived as just one of perhaps hundreds of dogs in a place where care and gentle ways were non-existent. She suffered this mental abuse day after day for a number of years as well as the physical trauma. No wonder she was utterly confused by all the love she now found herself surrounded by.

There was, and is, nothing commonplace about Twinkle or the way she challenges the casual assumptions of us and the wider world about what dogs think, or do, or need. From the first day I have found her endlessly bewitching and utterly bewildering – life with her is never dull. She seems determined to keep it so, for just when I think I may have her understood, she will pop out a new curiosity, behave in a weirdly unexpected way and make me think again. She is uniquely Twinkle.

For some dogs, the damage that is done to their bodies and minds during the years of abusive breeding is beyond complete repair. They simply cannot fully overcome their past. Heidi's story, told by her adopter Heather, illustrates the grip that the trauma can have on some poor souls who are not able to escape it fully, even in perfect homes with experienced families:

We had just lost one of our dogs and, coincidentally, we had an email from an excellent, small, London-based rescue, Pro Dogs Direct, bringing to our attention Heidi, a puppy-farm rescue. Bedraggled, hair unkempt and matted, she looked a sight. We visited her fosterer. Behind the settee where she had lived for the past three months – apart from going out to spend pennies and eat her food – Heidi cowered. My husband and I thought we were experienced with dogs, but we both felt that she was perhaps a 'bitch too far'. Severely traumatised, not reacting with the other dogs in foster, I really thought I had met my match. However, as we had brought all our dogs on the visit with us, I had the idea of bringing one of them, Tilly, into the house from the car. Immediately, Heidi came out from behind the settee, her tail up and wagging, and met Tilly as though greeting a long-lost friend. Gladys from Pro Dogs and the fosterer – both extremely experienced in the matter of rescue dogs – said they had never seen anything like it.

With trepidation we agreed to take her home, and Heidi came to live with us for over six years. During those six years she hated being picked up, stroked or touched. Every four months her coat grew unruly and teddy-bear-like until I took her to the vet so that I could cut it under sedation; she just could not bear me to do it when she was conscious. The condition of her teeth was terrible – she lost most of them within two years of coming to us.

But in her own way, Heidi had a wonderful time with us – she loved other dogs; cuddled and curled up with ours. She enjoyed her walks – it was a joy to see her running in the woods and fields where we live. Sometimes, but only rarely, if we were in our caravan on holiday relaxing, she would rest her chin on my legs if we were sharing the same berth, but as soon as she realised she was doing it, she would move away. All the time she was terrified of people, scuttling about to avoid them at all costs and she never got over this. We lost Heidi recently and she has left a huge hole in our family.

The reaction from Heidi to Tilly shows the comfort and reassurance that dogs from breeding places draw from other dogs. Without Tilly, Heidi would have been even slower in accepting her new life. At the time, Tilly had been with Heather and her family a couple of years when she met Heidi and brought her out of her fearful state, just far and long enough for Heather to decide to give her a chance at life. A puppy farm rescue herself, she had a big say in who her new family was to be, as Heather writes:

As we arrived at the fosterer's we were told that this five-year-old dog was extremely shy, did not do stairs, and was very traumatised. We went into the house and I went down the stairs into the basement kitchen to meet her. Then my husband followed. On spotting him descending, the little dog immediately started to go up the stairs and they met in the middle; they fell in love immediately! We called her Tilly in memory of our beloved, recently departed, Lilly.

Taking her home though, she was in shock. Rigid in my arms, she stared ahead, not looking right or left. Over the next few weeks she managed to get more confidence as she settled happily with our other dogs. But she was so unused to the outdoors, the grass, the birds, it appeared overwhelming at times and every time we took her out we were reluctant to let her off the lead as she seemed so frightened. The first time we did so, she was spooked and ran off, with my husband chasing her up a hill in the country park until she was successfully rounded up.

We still have Tilly, our beloved first rescue. Now fourteen years old and arthritic, she takes part of her daily walks in a doggy-pushchair looking all the while like the Queen of the May – a huge character with an even bigger appetite for food, especially sausages, who is still as besotted with my husband as he is with her.

4

Damaged Before Birth

No great mind has ever existed without a touch of madness.

– Aristotle

In her early weeks with us, Susie-Belle exuded an aura of controlled emotion, seemingly in a state of almost transcendent thought a lot of the time. Zoning out of everything around her was clearly her way of coping, but as she healed, so her true, wonderful personality began to break through the armour of restraint. These days, she wears her emotions bold and clear for all to see. There is nothing restrained about how she shows us what she needs, wants and feels. She happily clambers for attention, pushing through to sit ahead of her sisters in any queue for food. Never in my most optimistic daydreaming could I have pictured her paws on my knee, awaiting attention, now a daily shared delight, as my fingers scratch and tickle her happy little chin. As I watch her scrambling to keep up with Renae as they run in from the garden, where once she quietly crept in behind her bounding sister, I bask in her sunny personality shining bright and radiant, like I could never have hoped for. As a pot of freshly brewed coffee fills a house with a comforting, delicious aroma, so Susie-Belle's personality fills our home with warm joy. Only when she is in a busy or unfamiliar environment and she is unsure or tired does the old unwelcome bridle of controlled coping creep in.

But nowadays it is rare we see this; a combined result of us understanding her better and doing exactly what she needs to feel safe, plus of course, a much healthier, wholesome psyche of which she is now the proud possessor.

All of which makes her early months seem like another lifetime. But bringing Twinkle into our fold reminded us both of just how far Susie-Belle has travelled and how far away from happiness Twinkle was when she arrived. Not that Twinkle's traumatic behaviour resembled Susie-Belle's – they were markedly distinct, as Janet had warned. Susie-Belle's early days would see her sitting quietly, head hanging low, not appearing to notice all that much. In contrast, Twinkle, although not comfortable being in close contact with us, would sit with her head up high, watching our every move with a mixture of curiosity and vigilance, tipping over into hyper-vigilance here and there. At times, this would see her reacting to the slightest movement we made; at others, her watchfulness seemed more inquisitive. Occasionally she ventured out of her safe haven to lick our peanut-butter covered fingers when we attempted to show her that she did not need to be apart or separate herself to stay safe, that she had the whole house to explore when she was ready. But most of the time we just let her be. We allowed her to do exactly what she felt she needed to in order to bring herself to a mental state that would let her begin to function as a normal dog in a quiet, normal home. What must it be like to live in a world surrounded by newness, all of it confusing, most of it scary? It is hard for us to imagine. Harder still for the dogs who experience it.

It was a fine balance between allowing her the time and space she needed while avoiding the trap of not encouraging or coaxing her to come out into her new, safe world. Although I had learned to be patient through Susie-Belle's journey, I was conscious of the need to avoid anything developing akin to Heidi's months behind the sofa. At that stage, I did not know what Twinkle was capable of in terms of growth and normal behaviour, but I was sure I wanted to do all I could to help her live with us; properly live, not just exist in her self-selected safe place in our house. But I heeded all the signs that right then, for Twinkle, enjoyment in anything was inaccessible; she knew only that she needed to survive this new trauma. For trauma it undoubtedly was in her early days of freedom. She had brought anxieties, frights and terrors with her from the puppy farm and they were going nowhere just yet. So we accepted that we were terrifying to her. *I* was terrifying to her. There was nothing I could do but accept this and know it could only get better.

> Life begins on the other side of despair.
> – Jean-Paul Sartre

On the occasions I needed to handle Twinkle in the early months, this had to be done in a perfectly calm, peaceful frame of mind. Mine, that is – hers was in turmoil. With every action I made being keenly observed by a pair of wide, piercingly sharp, haunted eyes that missed little, I had to make sure nothing triggered alarm with Twinkle, for if it did, she would be off and away and out of my reach and we would need to abandon matters to allow her to settle. So while I made sure that I behaved quite normally and emanated quiet confidence – or at least I hoped I did – there had to be a constant awareness of how I was doing things to avoid her panicking. I became highly attuned to my own thoughts and movements, which is a good thing to develop in most aspects of life but essential with Twinkle.

There could be no hurrying sense or disorderly approach, as the slightest change to what she might expect would scupper success. There were some mornings where it took more than an hour to leave the house. Susie-Belle and Renae soon grew accustomed to our false starts at getting out, mooching around unperturbed as their new sister sometimes struggled to get the daily routines, or I did something to upset the peace. Answering the phone one morning as I was about to settle down next to her to put on her lead startled her and she was hot-footing it up the stairs to get away before I knew it, teaching me that multi-tasking and Twinkle are not a good idea. Initially putting a harness over her head completely petrified her. She hated it so I abandoned taking it on and off, leaving her wearing it till I solved the problem by using one that neatly slips and clips around her shoulders and waist, which she had no issue with at all, despite me handling her more when putting this on and taking it off. Over the head actions clearly disturbed her greatly. I didn't waste time imagining why, this was just one of many perplexing quirks Twinkle showed us in her early months.

There were times when she needed to be picked up – getting in and out of the car, for one, was impossible without me lifting her. Until we perfected how we did this together, in the early weeks, as I held her in my arms, cradling her rigid, unyielding, tight body to my chest, through my fingertips I would feel the rapid beating of her troubled heart. It was many, many months before human touch stopped causing Twinkle's skin to draw tight in alarm, rippling away from the unfamiliar, terrifying tactile sensation. Yet daily she would watch Renae fall into trance-like, half-comas of blissful pleasure as her back was stroked, her shoulders and ears massaged, and tummy tickled, but not be tempted to allow herself to sample the weird world of human touch that her sister so brazenly enjoyed. Twinkle sat, observant as ever, eyes not missing a moment of Renae's reverie, fraught with anxious trepidation that she might be next. Over a long period, way over a year of being with us, she slowly began to invite a little stroke of her ears; but only when she was at her calmest, first thing in the morning, would our gentle touches be reciprocated with a soft licking in return. But never for long. And not at all during the first year.

While Twinkle was battling her demons, I immersed myself in reading a variety of material, from academic literature to popular pieces. My need for information was in full spate and I read them all, gobbling them up in an intense effort to try to understand Twinkle's inner life better. I was driven by a blend of personal interest – when my curiosity gets tweaked by something, I want to know all I can about it – plus a desire to do the best I could to help our psychologically complex, damaged Twinkle. For while she was physically with us, mentally it was apparent that she was somewhere we could not yet reach. A great swaddling cloak of terrifying disturbance kept her from us, and us from her. But we both knew somewhere, deeply buried, was a happy Twinkle that one day we would reach. We knew that when she was ready we would sense the scrabbling, the sustained efforts at clambering free, and together we would be there to reach in and lift her up and out into the freedom of her new, bright, terror-free world. One day, one day.

My reading and digging around in academic tracts allowed me to feel I was kind of, in a way that satisfied my intellect if nothing else, on the way to reaching Twinkle. I thought if I knew more about what might be going on in her inner world, if that was even slightly possible to do, I would get to her quicker and bridge the gulf between her world and the one we offered, the one with a Twinkle-shaped space in it, just waiting to be claimed. What I discovered not only helped us to understand Twinkle a little better, it deepened my resolve to campaign as long as it takes and in any way I can to end the nasty breeding industry. An industry that damages puppies even before they take their first breath.

Although we will never know for sure, it is almost certainly the case that Susie-Belle and Twinkle were born in the miserable places where they were imprisoned for years. Their mothers, like they would be later, were undoubtedly malnourished and chronically stressed during their pregnancies. For their babies, this stress, together with poor nutrition, a cramped, awful environment and lack of caring, healthy human contact would have had multiple effects on how the genes of the puppies would behave. Known as epigenetics, this relatively new branch of veterinary (and human) medicine gives more disturbing insights into the terrible damage that puppy farming inflicts on those caught up in it. It describes how environmental factors can affect mammals at the level of their genes: a prenatal response to nutrients and environmental stressors, which means that what a mother eats and how she is stressed affects the wellbeing and health of her offspring in the earliest stages of their development, before they are even born. Twinkle never stood a chance of coming out normally into the world, neither the world of the puppy farm, nor ours.

The environment of a puppy farm is a stressful place for any living creature to be. None would be there by choice, except for the humans who operate them, who do choose to be complicit in, responsible for and blind to the suffering all around them. Terri, owner of a small rescue in the US that takes in ex-breeding dogs, describes a typical breeding place in her state, which is known as one of the worst places in the country for puppy mills:

> The noise at most mills is deafening, yet the owners walk around as if they are deaf. Most mill kennels are homemade. They consist of wire and wood. Wire floors to allow faecal matter to fall through, wire walls with wooden frames. Some are outdoors, behind buildings, but as they do not want to call attention to themselves, most hide the dogs away inside barns or sheds. Many of the dogs will never see sunshine or walk on solid ground. The odour in these buildings can make you drop to your knees and your eyes water, yet these dogs must live in it day in and day out. Feeding and care is often the responsibility of the owner's children, and is not always done daily. When I asked about empty water bowls, one man told me that even though it was scorching hot that day they would be watered after the children got home from school a few hours later.

In large-scale operations in the UK it is typical for dogs to be housed in disused agricultural sheds, in concrete pens, small kennels or cages packed into the sheds. But small-scale breeding places can be just as awful for the dogs, where they will be confined to sheds in back gardens, or dark crates in a house. The poor dogs will rarely be allowed to see daylight or experience fresh air. Some are kept in complete darkness for years.

For the breeding dogs like Susie-Belle and Twinkle, to stay confined for years in such a place is horrendous and any average, caring human being is capable of recognising this fact. Not the breeders. But as well as the obvious suffering and deprivation, there is a massive effect from the prison-like environment on the dogs' brain chemistry and development; it inflicts damage at the level of genetic tuning. Being in a chronically stressful situation affects the brain to the extent that it causes disruption in how genes make proteins and the brain grows. It is known that puppies reared in the dark – as is the case in some breeding places – have smaller brains than those raised normally. Limiting how the brain develops affects how learning and coping behaviours happen and this will continue way beyond puppyhood. Dogs whose origins are from bad environments are impaired before they even step out into the world and this leads to all kinds of behavioural issues they then have to cope with their entire lives as they live amongst us, inwardly battling the damage inflicted on them from their earliest moments of being. This must surely and deeply concern anyone who claims to care for animals.

But, just for a moment let us go back to the mother's pregnancy. At the time of giving birth, her deprivation has already affected the brains of her puppies – this is without even talking about in-breeding and hereditary issues, all rife in puppy farms. Although exact mechanisms are not completely understood by scientists, they do know that in mammals things like fear responses can be passed from mothers to fetuses. A breeding place is a fearful place for any creature and the puppies are born of mothers who know little else.

Once born, the puppies then spend the early days and weeks of their lives with little handling, no human love and no healthy stimuli to encourage healthy brain development. Puppy brains have more or less the same number of cells as adult brains but in puppies that exist in harsh, barren places, their brains do not grow; they are smaller than those of normal puppies. This is not down to poor cell proliferation as they have the same number, it is down to the connections between the cells, connections that occur through both external and internal signals. Remember the puppies raised in the dark and their smaller brains – without the stimulus of light, the brain connections to the eyes fail to develop correctly. Sights, smells and sounds all impact on brain growth and development.

Dogs that have little human contact before about five weeks of age, as in puppy factories, cannot recognise humans or have any concept of what they are. Without early, caring, tactile human contact, the immature puppy brains simply do not develop to recognise humans, let alone trust or relate happily to them. Good breeders know that to ensure healthy puppy development, new tactile sensations must be introduced in the early weeks at key stages of development. This is not training, it is stimulation for puppy brains so that they will continue to develop into normal dogs. Excellent breeders follow recognised time scales for introducing new sensations, such as toys to clamber over to develop spatial awareness. Gentle, slow, rhythmical massage and handling is also undertaken. None of this occurs in puppy farms or with bad – or even average – breeders who care about the money from the puppies and little else.

In a puppy farm, what is more likely is exposure to terrifying noises, sudden bursts of harsh activity as bowls or food are thrown into pens and cages. In the first four to five weeks of life, sudden noises or changes can permanently imprint themselves on puppies. Then just imagine how terrifying it is for puppies to be taken from their mothers at this stage, as they often are when being transported to be sold on by dealers. As they grow into adult dogs, their early weeks will have left a mark on their brains, and go on to affect how they live and learn in their new homes.

Taking puppies from their mothers before they have learnt to cope does not cause problems that are behaviourally rooted, although that is often how they are perceived; it is down to physical brain development, or lack thereof. The poor animals are completely unprepared to live as the companions they are supposed to be and want to be. The early damage done to their brains leads to problems such as noise reactivity, excessive barking, fearfulness in the home or outside on walks, aversion to humans, to strangers, to other dogs. Behaviourally they are compromised even before they take their first breath.

Of course, not all dogs are as damaged as others and many, given the right home environment, will be able to overcome much of their poor start. All dogs are individuals and within each breed there are differences; the fear response switches on at different times. For some it will be between six to eight weeks, in others it will occur around eight to ten weeks. But whenever the various behavioural systems and development stages occur, all dog brains will be damaged by a poor breeding environment. Most will not fully overcome it; they simply do not have the brain development to be able to. What they can do, given a good home, is learn to cope, and this is where dogs are remarkable. In view of all this, it is even more amazing that dogs like Susie-Belle and Twinkle, when given a chance to live in peace in normal, loving homes, are ever capable of healing in ways that we are fortunate to witness daily with them.

As I came across more of this information in my quest to know all I could about the brain and genetic damage Twinkle has had inflicted on her, I became a little obsessed. Whilst it helped me to understand better that her somewhat dramatic and inexplicable responses were so deeply rooted and beyond anything she could easily get over, I also struggled with the realisation of just how terrible it is for the dogs trapped in puppy farms and breeding kennels. Although I already knew it and had seen, read and heard enough horror stories of the conditions they exist in, when I went beyond the obvious and grasped the true extent of the psychological damage they experience it was a hard reality to manage.

I swung between black moments of despair, anger and sadness and hid them all from Twinkle as my angst would do nothing but harm her more. Michel and I have always tried to ensure little other than an air of calm confidence flows around her, Susie-Belle and Renae. We don't always manage it, light wafts of mild human anxiety do occur from time to time, but they are fleeting. As my brain filled with disturbing facts, looking into Twinkle's meltingly beautiful, wide open eyes staring back at me full of bewilderment and at times utter terror made my heart ache for her. Properly, physically ache.

As I loved her, but all she saw was me, a terrifying individual, the opposite of what I wanted to be for her, raw hatred towards her anonymous abusers burned at times within me. While they were still no doubt plying their lucrative, brain-damaging trade, Twinkle was left with a daily struggle to feel more than a few minutes of peace in her new world. But I refused to stay for long in that ugly mindset, knowing that simmering myself for hours in thoughts of how horrible some humans are would lead only to a pointless mashing of my mental well-being. Although it is tempting to do, if I give in to damaging, vicious emotions towards those behind the suffering not only of Twinkle, but of millions of dogs around the world, it lets their poison spread even farther. More is always going to be gained by remaining positive and trying to change what we can. This is what we aim for with Twinkle each and every day, and in the words of one of my favourite female writers, Maya Angelou:

> If you can't change it, change the way you think about it.
> *– Wouldn't Take Nothing For My Journey Now*

What I found as I deepened my research, with every paper and book I read that revealed how inhumane humans damage dogs for money, I became increasingly fired up to change things. I forced myself to replace venomous cogitating with a deep commitment to help bring an end to this terrible industry, one that can seem so entrenched in our current society it is hard to have any hope of destroying. But, I take heed of the wise words of Nelson Mandela: "It always seems impossible until it's done."

5

Could it Get Any Worse?

There may be times when we are powerless to prevent injustice, but there must never be a time when we fail to protest.

– Elie Wiesel

One morning I sat idly browsing the Internet not paying a lot of attention to what I was scrolling through. As my interest and commitment to animal rescue and puppy farming had started to take up a lot of my free time and most of my online newsfeed, the images sliding past me were of various animals in need, or pain, or some more fortunate ones in new homes, happily safe. Since Susie-Belle's story came out, the call of animal activism has properly awoken in me and what was once a brutal world away from my safe, placid, conventional one now fills much of my day in some form or another. But with the realisation that I cannot turn away from the vicious reality of commercial puppy breeding has come the serious need for me to maintain a personal balance between the vast amount of disturbing facts and images and a healthy share of more cheery news. As a relative newcomer to it, I recognised early on the need to pace myself with how much abuse I could engage with. If I fail to look for and appreciate the good, of which there is always plenty, as well as the bad, which can readily dominate, I feel too overwhelmed to cope. I know what my limits are for being able to manage to research, absorb and write about the reality of animal suffering, while not falling into thought paralysis and despair by total immersion in the full tragedy that many in our world inflict on animals. Living with our two survivors of the horrendous, wilful, abusive world of puppy breeding is sometimes enough reality for one day. But it is never long before I remind myself how much Twinkle and Susie-Belle endured for years, reflecting on their courage to stay alive, and soon enough I get back into the fray in whatever way I can to try and make a difference.

Just as I was thinking that particular morning that I should really get moving and take the dogs out for their walk, a headline and image came up that froze me to the spot. Plans for a walk went on hold as my eyes and awareness opened up to a whole new level of miserable exploitation in the breeding industry that I had never previously come across: dog auctions. The Internet link led to a US site advertising services across the Midwest of consignment and kennel dispersal auctions, the difference being the latter are breeding businesses closing down with all equipment and stock being auctioned – 'stock' including the poor dogs themselves. The consignment auctions are plainly livestock auctions, only it is not cattle or sheep being auctioned as we might be used to, it is companion animals; the dogs and puppies that should be living and loved in homes, not kennelled and confined and bred to within a whisper of death. And then sold off, still stuck in what amount to little more than rabbit hutches.

Could things get any worse for breeding dogs than being sold in auctions? The rest of the day I sat in a state of shocked disbelief as I researched what for me was the latest abomination I had come across being perpetrated by those intent on making every last penny from the dogs they confine and abuse. I got in touch with my contacts in the US to ask for more information and to try and determine how widespread the auctioning of dogs is. It seems that the auctions happen most weekends during the spring and summer months in the

Midwest, with tens of thousands of dogs passing through auctions every year.

Reading reports from rescuers who attend these nasty but legal events brought a rising feeling of sickness in my stomach as I sat and absorbed the horrific details. In many there can be hundreds of dogs sold, both individually to the highest bidder or in batches; puppies are often 'thrown in' with the price of the nursing mothers. The auctions take place in agricultural sheds with the dogs squashed in small crates or cages stacked round the space before being taken out and roughly displayed. Dispersal auctions are held at the breeding location and along with the wretched dogs being sold are the tiny, ramshackle, filthy cages in which they spend their entire breeding lives. The physical health of the dogs in all auctions is often poor and they are sold with missing teeth, eyes, limbs and toes, badly healed fractures and old injuries. In one auction catalogue I read listings for dogs with toes that had been chewed off by the mother; all this is stated and yet the buyers still buy. For these are auctions of breeding dogs and as one auctioneer was quoted as saying, missing eyes or teeth aren't a worry as "that's not where she breeds". Young puppies can fetch good prices as they have long breeding lives ahead of them.

Records from the few dogs that rescuers manage to obtain can show dogs passing through several auctions during their lifetimes, making money along the way for the humans involved in their suffering. A friend in the US, Karen, told me of her fostered breeding dog Libby, and her story illustrates a typical life for one trapped in this nightmare:

> Libby has a tattoo in one ear: 02 was her identity for twelve years. She is also microchipped which enabled us to trace some of her life and travels: she was bought and sold at auction several times and lived in three different states. Although her exact age was impossible to determine, it was estimated at between eight and

twelve when she was rescued. The number of litters she had during those years could be up to eighteen. They start breeding when they are around six months old and are bred twice a year; it's possible she may have had more litters. The day she was rescued she was due to be killed as she was ill with pyometra and could no longer have puppies. When the vet operated he could tell by scar tissue and her mammaries that she had undergone at least twelve pregnancies. When I picked her up at the rescuer's house she was a tiny, fragile, almost comatose three-pound malnourished Yorkie. Yorkies are in high demand in pet stores. It was thought she would never walk, having spent a life cooped up in a tiny space without exercise. Like many from the worst breeding places, she only has two teeth; this is typical as their drinking water is only available through rabbit water-bottle feeders attached to their cages.

During her time being fostered with Karen, Libby learnt to walk and run and despite being brutally debarked, how to use her voice. She experienced love for the first time in her life and today lives happily with her new family. Karen sees her regularly and describes Libby as the epitome of resilience and determination, enjoying every minute of her life at long, long last. Libby's full name, gifted to her by Karen, is Liberty, a beautiful name meaning 'freedom from captivity or slavery and the freedom to think'. So many years of pain and suffering had to be endured for her to be where she now is, but at least for Libby, her life will forever be one where she knows nothing but love, liberty and respect.

Although some states prevent auctions, many are entirely legal and licensed by the US Department of Agriculture and are places where only the most tenacious rescuers venture in to attempt to save dogs. Their efforts are cloaked in secrecy as animal welfare proponents are far from welcome, with the possible caveat that their presence can drive up prices if they are seen to try and save particular dogs. This account from Mindi Callison gives an insight into what goes on:

This was the first auction that I ever went to. I was 22 years old and in no way ready for what I was about to encounter.

A small group of friends and I drove almost two hours to attend a puppy mill auction. After years of bad USDA reports, they were leaving the business. Sadly for all of their 240 dogs (and a few puppies), they were being auctioned off like property instead of going to rescues.

This was a very intimidating experience, for sure, walking onto this property that I had read so many awful things about, not knowing if I would be kicked out immediately or if I would be hauled away because I couldn't keep my comments to myself. I was horrified at the place. There were several buildings that were not much more than sheds with runs on the sides of them. Most of the 'kennels' were in semi-trailers that had been turned into a giant dog house with outdoor access with wire cages lifted off the ground, with the dogs standing on the bare wire flooring.

There were around a hundred people in attendance and we were all given an eighteen-page packet with a list of the dogs that would be going on sale. This included their birth dates (if known), colour of dog, the last known pups, and whether or not the dog could possibly be pregnant. Seeing all of the dogs that needed saving was overwhelming, but we looked at the book and picked the dogs that we thought needed the most help. When the auction officially started, the items first being sold were the water bowls, some cage doors, and other little things like that.

Then the dogs were thrown on the auction table, and quicker than anything we were going through these dogs. The auctioneer decided to do more of a 'Dutch' style auction, where there were five of one type and the highest bidder could take his pick, take a few, or take the lot. Then the second highest bidder was offered a chance. After that the bidding would start all over again. I think this was done to try to deter the rescues from being able to get even a handful of animals.

While the bidding was going on, I noticed four guys in the back of the room who were all dressed pretty similarly. They were bidding on dogs, but never took a dog home. I feel they were there to drive the prices up if they noticed 'rescue type' people bidding.

As the poor animals came and went, I could see the terror on their faces. They were visibly shaken and terrified. Six-week-old puppies were held up and shown to the crowd, with the auctioneer stating 'they have their entire breeding lives ahead of them.' At one point in the auction, I watched as an assistant sarcastically saluted a dog as it was whisked away to its new life.

Most of the dogs were in pretty bad shape but none of this matters in the world of puppy mills and auctions. These were all products; property to be used, abused, and profited from. They were referred to by age, as in an ''08 model', like it was a car. It was pretty easy to tell who the breeders and rescuers were. Not that it made any difference to the auctioneer. Money was money. In the end, we were able to save a handful of lives, and I saw a few other rescues walking out with precious souls.

Now that I have been to this auction, I am forever changed. Since then I have been to several more and have witnessed many horrible things. I have seen too many evil people who use animals for profit.

Mindi now runs an educational campaign group, Bailing Out Benji, started when she was just twenty-one years old to raise awareness of puppy mills and other animal welfare issues.

Mindi's commitment to making things better for animals really took root when she saw a news story about a woman who kept her two Labradors and their eight puppies locked in a bathroom, malnourished and ill. When the charges were pressed there were only two counts of neglect instead of ten, which infuriated Mindi as ten lives were involved. This spurred her to research relevant state laws and in her opinion she found them wanting. She decided to campaign for better and has been doing so ever since. Along with other volunteers, she protests peacefully every weekend of the year at pet shops to educate the buying public about where the puppies have come from and the parents they leave behind in the puppy mills. During winter months in sub-zero temperatures, undaunted, they are out there making a difference; all the while the animals suffer, they will endure discomforts too.

As well as this, through her group's efforts dogs are saved from auctions and transported to willing rescues. Although the work of rescuers like Mindi to save dogs from the auctions brings criticism from some quarters, buying dogs for a pittance at a dispersal sale can hardly be judged to contribute to the massive scale of suffering that commercial-scale breeders inflict on dogs across the globe.

When asked what drives her, Mindi's response is simple: "People always ask me how I can have so much energy to do all of the stuff I do... I do it for my pets, for your pets and for the ones that leave the earth without ever knowing kindness."

I applaud the efforts of Mindi, Karen and others who dedicate their lives to making the world for dogs better, having witnessed at first hand the worst that humankind inflicts on them. In an age of social media rants, where people readily voice their hatred towards puppy farmers and bad breeders, spitting out words and vitriolic comments while rarely following through with useful action or engagement, it is good to know campaigners around the world like Mindi put words into action. Shouting on social media does little to help change things, although it makes those who rightly boil with anger feel better for a while. It is human action that the dogs need, not words alone. Actions based on an understanding of the issues that moves beyond the anger and hatred towards the perpetrators. Hatred is not enough, nor especially helpful as it blurs the way ahead. It is necessary to know how to make changes, and, like Mindi and her supporters, engage in the process. I am reminded of the words of Albert Camus when I think that it is deep, unconditional love for my dogs which fires me, and what drives the most effective campaigners is love, not hate:

> No great work has ever been based on hatred and contempt.

6

Engaging with Twinkle

You will never be happy if you continue to search for what happiness consists of. You will never live if you are looking for the meaning of life.
— Albert Camus

Like her sister Susie-Belle, Twinkle came to us with a healthy appreciation of food, which got markedly stronger as she enjoyed the full range of culinary delights served up daily. It helped us no end to connect with her on at least some level, especially in the calm, controlled environment of home, but even this took a long time. It was shocking at first to see how she could not bring herself to take a treat from our hands, for an action so normal for most dogs to be a cause for suspicion, or worse, naked fear, brought her reality sharply into focus. The reluctance some dogs show accepting food offerings in this way can result from past experiences where they have been lured by their captors in the breeding places, only to be grabbed when they get within reach; or because some other awful action resulted from them falling for the treat and allowing themselves to trust a human, even for a second. It is astounding that dogs tricked by humans and ill-treated for years ever do let themselves risk being close to any once they are rescued. But they do and for that I rejoice.

So inside the house, where distractions were minimal, we worked on getting her to recognise a proffered treat as simply that, a treat. Nothing more was attached to it, aside from our love and hope that one day she would accept this as her norm. It took many patient attempts some days to help her accept a treat without it inducing a dose of the Twinkle jitters. We never pushed it, and delicately weighed up each tiny sign she gave us as to whether to abandon, or patiently sit things out. Michel and I trust our instincts with our dogs, and having done a fair amount of work on understanding canine body language, I allow my intuition to guide me with what Twinkle can and cannot manage on every step of the journey we are sharing. I craved the day when not only would Twinkle take a treat from me in a state of perfect ease and enjoyment, but that she might sense it as her rightful due, a reward for being the remarkable survivor she is.

Susie-Belle certainly does these days, throwing looks that only a fool could fail to read as *Where's mine? I'm rather deserving, you know?* if she fails to snaffle a snack before Renae gobbles it up. Or I make her wait her turn and her head swivels sharply left, then right, then back to me accusingly, astounded that first one, then the other sister gets their biscuit before hers is offered. It is remarkable how often Susie-Belle places herself in the middle of her sisters; not to the side, certainly never at the back, but in the middle, so she won't be missed out and may, just may manage to snatch an extra treat on its way to one of her sisters' lips. Anthropomorphising? Probably. There again, I could be right.

Rewarding Susie-Belle, and Twinkle if only she lets me, for just being here, themselves, happy, is the least we can do, for this is how I view all dogs who endure what they have in their lifetime: glorious, unique beings. We owe it to them to make them feel no less than the remarkable, treasured creatures we are honoured to share our lives with. We have so much to make up to them and Susie-Belle now soaks up all on offer; whether it be cuddles, food or company, all are greedily enjoyed. But it would be many months before the occasions that Twinkle would do the simplest action – accepting a treat directly from our hands – outnumbered the times this act spooked her. Even today, over two years out of the puppy farm, there are times when an outstretched hand bearing the gift of a tasty morsel is suspect and off she'll shoot to her bed, foregoing something delicious in favour of her peace of mind.

After a couple of months with us, we recognised that behind the glaringly obvious fear of almost everything and everyone, there lay within Twinkle an incredibly bright, intelligent dog. Due to the overt drama of her responses to day-to-day things that most dogs would not really notice, let alone react to, it took us a while to look beyond this to find her true character. A character which had been blighted for years by the life she had been forced to live, but which had not been totally killed off. We began to see subtle glimpses of the real Twinkle as she started to accept and understand the routines of our life together. Where we saw hyper vigilance one day, on another, if she was in a calmer state this seemed more like keen observation. Her sharp eyes never missed a moment of activity within the home and where on a bad day it could lead to super-charged reactions of flying round the house in a panic, or into her bed, tucking herself deep into the corner in a tight bunch of nervousness, on better days, she would simply follow what her sisters were doing, watching and learning how to be a dog in a home, not a machine in a breeding shed. A beautiful symbiotic bond between the three dogs began solidly forming as Twinkle drew from each of them what she needed to help her adjust to her new world. It is sad to think that a world of simple care and love can be one that some dogs have to learn and struggle to live in, one that is far from normal for them. What a shameful truth that is to lay at the feet of the people who cause them to suffer.

As it dawned on us that if we put aside all the drama, angst, and at times, alarming behaviour, there lay a clever dog desperately learning in her own way, what was needed in order to survive in her scary new life – for it is all about survival nothing more, to a dog from her background –

I decided the best thing we could do would be to look past Twinkle's fears and attempt to engage her intelligence. I knew that this may be only partially possible, as she could so quickly find herself in a terror-filled maelstrom out of what seemed to us, nothing. The slightest wrong action or movement could stir all manner of agitation in Twinkle where only a second earlier she appeared almost calm. Even today, we can never truly describe Twinkle as existing in a state of real peace. On her good days, of which there are increasingly more, there is always an alertness lurking just below what seems a tranquil veneer. On other days, the veneer is not there and Twinkle's tensions are blatantly still present.

When we realised how bright she is, I knew that if we could redirect some of the frantic energy she expended on fretting about what was going on or what was about to happen into learning a new behaviour or action, just something simple, it may switch her brilliant brain into a different mode, even if this was only for a few seconds. I hoped that even if it was fleeting, a thought process and resulting action – receiving a delicious treat – that was not fuelled by fear or anxiety but by intelligence, by calculation and cognition, would stretch her mind in ways that could only be good. It was worth trying to sow some confidence in Twinkle's mind that she could create good things in her world, if only we could learn to communicate amongst ourselves better. Lessons were in order all round.

So, during our Easter break in France, where we had few distractions and plenty of time, I decided to teach Twinkle to sit, but, and this would be her real challenge, to accept a reward for doing so. This may seem an easy thing to do – it is after all the first thing we teach puppies and they do it because they want the reward. But with Twinkle, accepting food directly from us or indeed just kindness, was something she struggled with. I had to learn that teaching a dog with such a high level of anxiety and outright fear requires a difference in approach. The method I had used to teach puppy Renae, pretty standard puppy training fare, involved me gently moving my hand back above her head and while her nose lifted, as if by magic, she sat her plump puppy bottom down awaiting the tasty reward. Easy. Renae, like most puppies, had it mastered within minutes. Now try it with a dog for whom a hand going anywhere near them, let alone above their head, is a trigger to run and this technique is soon discarded as useless; I abandoned it within the first few minutes of Twinkle's first lesson. There was even less chance of me gently touching her backside to encourage a sit as Renae had occasionally needed.

As Twinkle was taking most of her cues from Susie-Belle and Renae, I decided she was only ever going to learn with their assistance. So, with a plate full of smelly, tasty treats and them sitting like baby birds, mouths at the ready, they both must have rejoiced at the morning they had that day; acting as Twinkle's teachers, they were fed treat after treat as they obediently sat, stood, sat to command, with Twinkle keenly studying and wondering at this new way to spend time with humans. Eventually, after much watching, looking at me and over at her sisters, moving away and coming back, thinking, working it out, Twinkle managed to do several sits. She was so sweet when she did each one, tentatively lowering her bottom, eyes never leaving my face. What was even more delightful – and I had to curb the urge for exuberant celebrations for that would have ruined the moment in an instant – was her moist nose, softly nudging my fingers to release a treat into her slowly opening mouth. There was no frenzied snatch and grab in the way she usually engaged. The controlled taking of her reward following a specific action was a transformation that was beautiful to witness. This is what I had hoped the activity might help her with: getting her brain to operate beyond instinctual reactions. She was learning that she could create an outcome. Perfect.

We had several sessions through that first day and each time we tried it was back to the beginning, with

Twinkle looking cautious but interested, then after a few demonstrations from her sisters, joining in. The biggest challenge for her was not in knowing what the hand signal and new word meant – she got that quickly as I knew she would – rather, it was trusting me enough to take her reward when she sat. It was apparent that she had quickly mastered what the activity was all about, but overcoming her mistrust of a person nearby, even one with a treat in hand, was the bigger achievement. Initially, she needed to be in exactly the same place each time to do it. When I moved to another room and tried it with her, she grew too suspicious and could not settle into the activity. But back in the kitchen where we had first perfected it, she did it straight off. It was fascinating to see how the slightest variation caused her enough disturbance to scupper the fragile confidence that allowed her to sit and take the treat.

As we were doing so well, I kept the activity going on and off throughout the day, fuelled by rich, tasty treats to keep Twinkle enthused. However, conscious that neither Renae nor Susie-Belle really needed rewarding for each sit and their waistlines could certainly be spared the deluge of treats, I switched to carrot sticks for them, only for Susie-Belle to promptly stop assisting. Instead, with some disdain she spat each carrot piece out, and stood and stared at me with a look of disappointment that I expected her, Susie-Belle the Gourmet, to be rewarded with crudités while Twinkle was served sausage.

Susie-Belle's gluttony had moved up a notch since Twinkle had come into the household. She was always at the front of any food queue and in her charming, determined way, would ensure she was never overlooked or left to last as meals or snacks were given. She has always been such a sweet, shyly retiring dog but with Twinkle's arrival, her confidence soared and she was soon as demanding as any other dog who likes their food. This has only got keener as time has passed and these days out on walks she is first to receive a slice of liver cake, a delicious speciality of our friend Kate that Susie-Belle cottoned onto after her first mouthful of this particular delight. When we are walking with her, Kate can barely move a few steps without looking down to see Susie-Belle's upturned face, pleading for more. She has mastered a look of pure food lust and uses it with unerring success. When I came across the old English verb 'to groke', which according to Mark Forsyth, author of the wonderful book *The Horologicon*, means 'to stare wistfully at somebody while they are eating in the hope that they will give you some of their food', I realised it is a word perfectly crafted for Susie-Belle. Few are immune to her groking and as she knows it produces such effortless results, she practises it at every opportunity. The little schnauzer who once would timidly hang her head low in the hope of appearing invisible to humans can now out-groke any dog when food is about. If groking was an Olympic sport, I would be polishing Susie-Belle's medal collection.

To think that I had once wondered whether bringing Twinkle home might set Susie-Belle back... I could not have been more wrong in that thought. It was a wonderful surprise to see Susie-Belle assert her place in our little ménage, especially when we began teaching and rewarding Twinkle. Whether it is angling for a treat, awaiting a meal, or just wanting some affectionate attention, she is there, at the front, demanding we notice her first. There is now no sign of her previous preference for hiding at the back, trying not to be noticed, pretending to be small or not really there and there is certainly never any hint of cowering or hanging her head. On home territory or surrounded by familiar faces and friends, that old Susie-Belle went long ago, and she has grown into her role of big sister to Twinkle, showing her that by sitting at the back being coy, she will miss out. Most mealtimes Susie-Belle demonstrates that it is a jolly good idea to bounce up and down in the kitchen the moment that food preparation begins, twisting and twirling in her distinctive, uncoordinated, awkward way around my feet. Or, if that fails to produce the desired dish of delights, she gives a perfect performance for her sister of staring intently at me, with her bottom wiggling hard, docked tail furiously twitching, making herself impossible to be ignored. Delightfully, once we started teaching Twinkle, she showed her sister that on hearing the word 'sit' it is always best to plonk her bottom down, with shoulders spread wide, head held high, eyes brightly shining, and if done quickly enough not only will one tasty treat be the reward, but by being in pole position, there is every likelihood of grabbing another as it is offered across to Renae, who is always so slow with taking food. Although in some dogs Susie-Belle's cheeky antics and high food drive may not be desirable, in our house it is all good and her soaring confidence has been an amusing, unexpected spin-off to Twinkle's development; thankfully, Renae refrained from following suit, and most of the time she remains the calm dog she has matured into, acting as a welcome bulwark against too much canine chaos around food.

By the time we returned to the UK after the Easter break and many days of practice, Twinkle was reliably sitting to command and taking her rewards most of the time. There were still issues that needed to be worked on with it, for example, I had to time it correctly to avoid her rushing off in a state of high suspicion without her reward, having done what for many dogs is the challenge, the perfect sit. I could not show any enthusiasm when rewarding her, as that immediately triggered alarm. The whole activity always had to be done calmly and with the assistance of at least one of her sisters, whom she would mimic. While with regular dogs the sit itself is the purpose of the exercise, with Twinkle it was more about her understanding that if she engaged with us in a calm and controlled way, nice things followed. For her at this stage it was always food as nothing else would work; excited, cheerful voices, toys, cuddles, all the other tools and rewards used with puppies were obsolete. They would have the opposite effect than intended. So where it is not necessary to reward puppies with food every single time an activity succeeds, with Twinkle her development was so fragile at this stage that variation had to be introduced exceedingly slowly and offering a food reward to mark an action was the only way to connect with her. If there were any changes to what she was expecting to happen, she would revert back to her old self. Even tiny variations, if she was not prepared, affected her, which might be as simple as me crouching, instead of standing; or kneeling, not crouching; or using an open palm to offer the food if previously she had taken it from my fingers; a simple change could find us starting from scratch once again. But we were pleased to have found at least something that we could build on with her in the coming months where she was clearly using her brain. It was great to have her seemingly content to watch and learn, rather than watch so that she could be ready to run.

I took heart that after just a few months we were making some progress, steadily learning how Twinkle might reach a state of happiness in her new life. Although we rarely understood what she was thinking, and a lot of guesswork governed how we went about each day keeping her on the road to living as a regular dog, we saw that however she was doing it, she was learning that life might, just might, be worth living. For me in particular, it was rewarding to know that the simple things we did with Twinkle were making a difference, helping her to roll forward to a better, calmer disposition. Simple routines, an orderly day with good experiences and generally, bar the odd incident, we got through each one with us all feeling fine. Although I have a restive need at times to understand things in great detail, to overthink and analyse, as Twinkle's responses to us grew clearer and steadier, I let that go. I grew to understand that it really would never matter that I might not understand what goes on in her mind. It is enough to know that we can most certainly, fulsomely, love her without understanding her and what she has gone through to be as she is.

7

Is that a Wink, Twinkle?

Hope is the thing with feathers
That perches in the soul
And sings the tune without the words
And never stops at all.
        – Emily Dickinson, *Hope is the Thing With Feathers*

Just as we did with Susie-Belle when she arrived, we tried hard with Twinkle to give her a varied life, picking up different experiences along the way. We firmly believe that it helps our dogs to move out of their hideous past if we can provide many good memories for them through good days out, meeting new dogs and the company of lots of kind people. The latter is particularly critical, as their history with humans is something no dog should be made to experience, let alone remember. But it was not straightforward with Twinkle as her responses to things are more complicated and unpredictable than Susie-Belle's. Plus, just the practical challenges of handling three dogs, two with particular needs, meant we did things at a different pace; we adapted routines and activities and at times, avoided things we might have contemplated doing with Susie-Belle. Keeping all dogs safe and happy always takes priority over any plans we may have. It was not at all uncommon, especially in the first eighteen months, for us to plan a day out and then, with her showing signs of stress or erratic behaviour, have to abandon it to give her time and space to settle. And then there were days where I would be concerned that it could all be a bit too much for the fragile bonds of confidence we were building, only to have her sail through like nothing ever worried her, that she was really a confident, sassy little schnauzer, and she was only joking with us about being a bag of nerves.

An example was the day I took her for her first proper eye examination. She had been with us for over a year and at times I thought that she just did not seem to see me, or was unable to focus correctly. The more I thought I noticed it, the more it started to concern me, as miniature schnauzers can develop a range of serious eye problems, some of which lead to blindness. Before Susie-Belle came to us she had received cataract surgery and she has an ongoing 'dry-eye' condition which requires constant treatment, and while Susie-Belle has always been wonderful with receiving any veterinary attention, the thought of Twinkle being happy with close contact for an eye assessment did not fill me with confidence. I delayed it for some while before deciding eventually that I had to get on and do the right thing for her, even if the experience was not going to be easy – on her, me or the vet.

So the appointment was booked at our brilliant veterinary clinic, where I have complete confidence and trust in everyone. We arranged a session with the specialist eye vet out of regular hours so it was quieter and Twinkle would not be under any extra stress. This particular eye examination involved Dr Savov peering directly into her eyes for several minutes at a time, and repeatedly over the course of about forty-five minutes using his special instruments, his face only inches from hers. As it had taken me the usual routine of calmly, quietly waiting for her to settle in her chosen place in the house to allow me to put her harness on, before she steeled herself ready to allow me to lift her into the car for the short drive to the clinic, I stood agog watching her with Dr Savov. All the routines with her that we needed to stick to, the calm confidence I summoned to help Twinkle through her days, seemed to occur in a parallel dimension as I stood watching her. There she sat, calmly perched on the examination table, with a stranger looming towards and away and towards her again. Extraordinarily, she looked for all the world like a seasoned show dog, not fidgeting about or seeming to mind in the slightest being closely examined. She clearly had no intention of letting a trifling thing like her usual crippling anxiety interfere with her afternoon with the charming Dr Savov, who must have thought I was making it all up about the careful handling his special afternoon patient would require. I could not believe that she was genuinely calm in those circumstances; I know the difference between her shutting down and freezing in fear, I've seen enough of that to recognise it. After the months I had watched Twinkle, the more subtleties I saw and could quickly sense the tiniest of cues that all was not good with her. No, that was not what was happening, although how she perceived her day right then was a mystery. Perhaps it was as simple as thinking this was just another nonsensical thing that her human family decided to do with her and it was all quite okay and there was no need to do anything other than sit still. Twinkle well and truly flummoxed me that day.

> If I had a world of my own, everything would be non-sense. Nothing would be what it is, because everything would be what it isn't. And contrary wise, what is, it wouldn't be. And what it wouldn't be, it would. You see?
> – Lewis Carroll, *Alice's Adventures in Wonderland*

Twinkle was, and still is, a pickle of a personality to fathom at times, determined to keep us endlessly guessing at what she may be thinking. Not wanting to break whatever magical spell Dr Savov had woven, I stayed quiet, inwardly smiling as she looked over his shoulder at me. I almost expected to see a cheeky wink escape one of her beautiful, big black eyes. Eyes that are pools of inky dark memories, but which are, thankfully, quite healthy. I like to think the world gives us simple daily miracles and this was one of them.

Expect nothing. Live frugally on surprise.

– Alice Walker

Getting Twinkle used to traffic noise has been essential as we live in a busy part of the UK, and I started her off, same as Susie-Belle, by walking in our high street in the early mornings as it was just coming to life, before it got too hectic or noisy. The first few trips were slow, with a lot of stopping and looking around. It was amusing seeing how she would pause at the closed shop windows, curiously peering in; some were given particularly careful inspection as she walked right up, nose to the glass, eyes wide. Perhaps it was her reflection causing her such fascination; whatever it was, it was rather sweet to see her enjoy the novelty of a high street wander in the early morning. It was all wildly different to the barrenness of the puppy farm where she had spent too much of her life, trapped. Each trip outdoors was an opportunity to stimulate her senses, to give her something, indeed lots of things to think about besides her fears.

Twinkle came alive outside of the house. She became a dog, interacting with the world the way dogs do: through her nose, ears and eyes as they were bombarded with new stimuli. I could almost feel her – with the novelty of each new sight, sound and smell, she would grapple with it at first, then study it, ponder it, let it run through her busy, bright mind, then gently, slowly, align herself to this new sensation and be ready to move on to the next one.

While Twinkle admired each window, Susie-Belle and Renae patiently stood and waited for the walk to continue. What they must have thought of their new sister's approach to walking can only be wondered at. She showed a side to her personality then that as time has gone on, has become much clearer to us: she is a fabulously curious creature.

Her curiosity is boundless and she never misses a chance to stand, stare and watch. As soon as we saw how it helped her to grow, it became a truly beautiful thing to see her taking things in, knowing that for her, it was the first time she had seen something, whether it was as simple as waves at the beach, the flow of a river or birds in the garden. But all the while, behind her wonderment lurked a pernicious presence; out of apparently calm curiosity, alarming panic could swiftly erupt, often with no obvious warning.

Traffic sounds I knew were scary for Twinkle and any sudden noise could easily result in her flipping around on the end of her lead in a panic. On Janet's sage advice she wore a securely fitting harness which I attached to her collar, so if she managed to flip out of the harness, she would still be safely secured. I am glad I took the advice as more than once Twinkle the Little Houdini wrestled herself out of the harness in a frenzied few seconds, startling the living daylights out of me. We had never needed to fear this with Susie-Belle as her responses were completely different, much more controlled and easily managed. Having two dogs with such different responses truly reminded me of the uniqueness of dogs generally, but with survivors of commercial breeding in particular, how nothing can be assumed. There can be great variations in the kind of place that they come from, the degree of inhumanity they are exposed to and the abuse they suffer, with some places not being especially cruel but not what those who know better would want for our companions. Whereas Twinkle and Susie-Belle clearly endured the nastiest end of the breeding environment spectrum, the experience of Jan with her dog Dolly illustrates that not all survivors bring quite the level of trauma with them when they get to live normal lives. At the time of contacting me, Dolly had been with Jan and her other dog, Dexter, around five months:

Dolly has done so well. She is affectionate, cuddly and relaxed and walks beautifully on her lead although

75

I have to use a slip lead as she can suddenly panic. I doubt that this propensity to react anxiously to some outside stimuli will ever stop. She and Dexter love each other so much and cuddle up in the same bed together. They really enjoy their long walks, snuffling around and exploring together. Dolly doesn't understand toys or play as such. However, she often runs around with other dogs who are playing and sometimes she dashes alongside Dexter when he chases his ball. She loves all kinds of walks, whether at the country park, the woods or on the beach, and she will even splash happily through the rock pools. She is a bit apprehensive of new people but once she feels confident you would never know she had any issues. This makes me hope she wasn't actually abused although she hates being picked up and still doesn't really like people walking behind her. She is such a smiley, happy girl and so evidently loves her new home and her life – it is no doubt anthropomorphising but it seems to me that she appreciates every moment with gusto. She is like my shadow, always by my heel or snuggling next to me.

Dolly's weight is now normal and she has muscle tone, whereas she was like a roly-poly jelly when I adopted her; although I don't think her tummy pouch from all those litters of puppies will ever go. She takes most things in her stride but is nervous of young children and reacts to unexpected loud noises. She takes her lead well from the confident Dexter – he is virtually bomb-proof and adores kids and all people. He teaches her not to be afraid and he takes a lot of comfort from her too. I've noticed she often curls around Dexter to 'protect' him despite the fact he is big and athletic and she is tiny!

She did very well on a recent trip we made to London and went for walks on Hampstead Heath which was Dexter's old stomping ground before we moved to the coast. I can easily forget she is not a 'normal' dog most of the time but sometimes I am reminded of her background. For example, we were walking not too far from the Royal Free Hospital in London and an ambulance whizzed past and suddenly put on its siren. Unfortunately my friend, who was leading Dexter, had just dashed across the road, and without her comforting older brother to help calm her, Dolly was petrified and tried to bolt. It was terrifying as we were on an island between two busy roads but, thanks to the slip lead, I was able to hold on to her and the incident was quickly forgotten. On that same trip Dolly came with me, my friend and Dexter to have lunch at the Greenberry Café in Primrose Hill. Dolly lay under the table next to Dexter – a veteran of cafés and restaurants since he was a pup – and she accepted her special treat and bowl of water from the waiter like any other pampered pooch, receiving many compliments from fellow diners and the staff. It was hard to believe that four months earlier she still lived on the puppy farm and was not even familiar with clean drinking water, let alone being spoiled like this in a stylish eatery.

Dolly's story is a perfect example of successful adoption and how a dog, given a chance at life, can embrace it wholeheartedly. Since adopting Dolly, Jan has become a strong advocate for ending puppy farming and in one of our exchanges made these salient points:

I have often chatted to fellow dog walkers about Dolly and have a chilling sense from some of them that it is not always that they did not know what puppy farming is (although perhaps they turned a blind eye on how bad it can be) but that they had found a way to disregard or even accept it as the price of the bargain dog of their choice at the time that they want it. The concept of choosing breeds and having them at the ready, wherever and whenever someone wants, should not be acceptable.

It is like being able to buy cheap goods on the high street. There is always a consequence to being able to buy a sequined top for a few pounds, just as there is to being able to go online or into a shop and get the breed of your choosing entirely at your convenience.

This is one of the major issues that we face as campaigners: reaching the hearts and changing the minds of the many; those who choose not to see what lies behind their puppy purchases. It is this wilful ignorance that fuels the market and makes it profitable for the puppy farmers to continue doing as they do. While some people genuinely do not realise what is happening today in puppy breeding, in an age that drowns in information and where social media spreads the truth more easily than ever before, the validity of Jan's astute commentary is beyond question. In the absence of effective legislation and poor enforcement of what there is, it is vital that we touch the consciences of individuals and show them how their behaviour keeps the trade going. But it is challenging to achieve this when a consumer-driven society currently thrives; where things can be wanted one day, bought the next, only to be discarded soon after. Removing pets from what is, for the animals involved, a nasty modern affliction – shallow consumerism – has to be a priority for all of us who care.

8

Near Calamity

*Never give up, for that is just the place and time
that the tide will turn.*

– Harriet Beecher Stowe

Out and about with Twinkle in the early weeks of her new
life, things quickly became tricky if she panicked, so we kept
her on a long training lead for quite a while for her own safety.
She was responding well to food cues when she was calm but
if she was startled, which might be caused by something as
simple as a leaf blowing around her feet, the ensuing panic
could rapidly engulf her, sweeping away any interest in food.
It was some time before we felt confident enough to let her off
the lead, much longer than with Susie-Belle.

When we did so, I used a tip from a behaviourist who
suggested attaching her to Renae; that way it kept Twinkle
safe as Renae's recall and reliability is solid. It worked
brilliantly as Twinkle has always, from day one, been happy
to trot alongside Renae, following her confident direction.
Renae – patient, tolerant, trusting – seemed not to mind
having her new sister attached and it was an ideal method for
Twinkle (and us) to build some confidence. It was by no means
Twinkle alone whose nerve might wobble as she grappled her
way to finding enjoyment in her new life; I regularly reminded
myself that her unpredictability was all part of the interesting
journey I had committed us to. I vowed that whatever we did,

we were in it together and she and I and Michel would learn as we went, our bond strengthening along the way. While I never once had doubts that we had done the right thing in bringing her to us, there were occasional incidents when sharing a normal life with Twinkle, giving her the freedom to run at liberty, unrestrained, did not go to plan.

We have never wanted to keep our dogs leashed whilst out and about any more than a sensible minimum to keep them safe. For me, seeing dogs running freely, bounding round parks, through woods, across open landscapes and beaches has always been a pleasure. Even more so when I know they once lived being denied even the faintest breath of liberty. The increasing trend these days for tighter controls and restrictions on where and how dogs can enjoy the space we allow them to share in our society saddens me deeply. To think that until relatively recent years, dogs happily spent their days wandering round villages, mooching around meeting their friends, being seen and accepted as part of their local community, roaming happily and returning home after a day spent being dogs. Of course, the dangers of busy roads, frantic lives and hectic environments has put paid to these natural joys for many humans as well as dogs, but a boring life spent cooped up indoors and kept permanently on leads on walks is not one I will settle for with my dogs.

Since living with two that once knew no freedom whatsoever, I feel even more strongly that they deserve to enjoy the world they are now a part of, without unnecessary restraint. With us, they have full emancipation: if they want to run, they run; if they choose to putter and sniff the ground and air and all things odorous, they do this; their unshackled bodies, minds and spirits are theirs, and theirs alone to do with as they wish. It holds powerful symbolism for Michel and me seeing Susie-Belle and Twinkle doing just as they please when we are out together, unleashing them as soon as we can. Of course, being the responsible guardians that we are, *ahem,* when I say do as they please, we live as regular members of society and we, as humans, obey the rules. Most of the time. Thankfully, their doggy manners are good and they are rarely a nuisance, or bother to others. A rare benefit of their unusually cruel but dog-centred background does mean they understand other dogs well, their time on this earth with dogs being so much greater than with humans, and interactions are mostly a pleasure for all. My dogs are normal with their own kind; humans muddle things, and left to meet and mingle as dogs do, they are happy.

I make no judgements on how anyone else walks their dogs; every circumstance is unique and there can be excellent reasons to keep a dog on a lead. Some good friends do exactly this. I just know that for us, a life as free as we can make it is what our dogs will enjoy. Mary Oliver, the Pulitzer-prize-winning poet, writes beautifully on dogs and these words from her wonderful book *Dog Songs* resonate with me:

> The other dog – the one that all its life walks leashed and obedient down the sidewalk – is what a chair is to a tree.

As our home in the UK lies in one of the most heavily populated parts of the country, it can be tricky to find places that offer our dogs the safe freedom of unleashed walks, the joy of which I feel is their due. But we do it each day and sometimes will travel miles to find a good place to explore. Twinkle is always happiest whilst out and about and since having three dogs and the peculiarities of Twinkle to take into account, we have found some gems of places that are worth the extra drive. Unlike Susie-Belle, who favours staying close on walks, Twinkle from the start has been eager to head off exploring the environment, nose twitching, ears alert, eyes scanning the scene. I will not deny her this pleasure. In the early months, when inside the house, her cruelly docked stump of a tail would stay tucked out of sight, unseen for hours, a bristly barometer of the unrelenting anxiety that burdened her, but, as soon as we got walking somewhere good, up it would happily stand. The simple sight of her pert bottom topped by the scrappy remains of her tail, sashaying away down a track, still brings a smile to our faces.

To see her transform into behaving like any normal, happy, regular dog enjoying a walk and run has always been an utter joy. It does however mask a myriad of complicated emotional issues that strangers meeting her have no idea about. In the past, it was only if people witnessed us preparing to get her back into the car that they grasped some of the problems she carried around with her. The ritual dance we did each time to get her to stay within arm's reach, to still her anxious circling if we approached too quickly to clip her back on the lead; the light-footed side step she superbly executed when a hand reached down, backing away, eyes watching for our next move, steadily working herself up into a whirling pool of panic. All this a daily dance, the Twinkle Two-Step; she had it perfected and we learnt it well. Then, when she was ready, I would lift her into the car, her front legs gripping, her back rigid, claws digging in like powerful talons, driven by raw terror at being handled. This went on for months and months. But then, suddenly, or so it seemed, we reached an understanding, Twinkle and I. If I stood beside the open car boot, bending gently down without looking at her, she would spring directly from the ground, propelling herself with sheer determination to get the deed done, into my waiting arms. I then slowly and calmly released her tight, coiled body out of my arms into the relative safety of the car. Once we both learnt that this was the way to end a walk – on Twinkle's terms, which is always fine by me – it became a skilful display of acrobatics she mastered with elegant grace. That was unless she started her leap upwards into arms that weren't ready, taking me by surprise, resulting in an ungainly flop back to the ground, which was politely ignored by us both as I smartly prepared for her second jump up and all was back to normal. Our normal.

These days, after a million and one lifts into the car

on her terms, in her own time, where I gather her up in one perfectly choreographed, practised movement, holding her tight, I sneak the opportunity to enjoy a cuddle, one where Twinkle is perfectly relaxed. She is most at ease in my arms when she has leapt into them to get into the car. She knows this is on her terms. She is in control. And as I snuggle her close for a few seconds, sometimes longer, I massage her floppy ears and into each whisper, "Twinkle, Twinkle, little star, how we wonder how you are." Heaven forbid anyone hears me.

Since teaching her to 'sit' at Easter, we had continued to strengthen our bonds and increase Twinkle's responsiveness to us, gradually finding more ways to communicate and relay our wishes; hers to us, ours to her. We were learning as fast and as much as she was about how to live together. In our small world, in the first months, we employed a range of measures to help her cope with the daily routines and to minimise Twinkle's stress. As soon as we were ready to start letting her off the lead, we still kept attached a long line that trailed, which could be stepped on as needed to keep her still, or safe. Although having a filthy and often wet lead on Twinkle was a minor inconvenience (to us, not her – she didn't seem to notice it), it did mean she could enjoy the freedom of running with Renae and friends, off exploring, and still be capable of being put back on the lead as required.

Through the first summer we all grew in confidence and by autumn she was reliably trustworthy when we were out, with only occasional glitches, just enough to remind us that Twinkle's inner world was in constant flux. The most important command to keep her safe was 'sit', as this meant she stayed still long enough for us to approach to clip her lead on. Teaching her 'stay' proved near impossible while we were out so those lessons were swiftly ditched and we just got her to sit instead. It worked: I was happy, she was, well, perhaps happy is a stretch, but at least sitting, she was safe. On walks, we kept commands simple and avoided surprises. Deviations from what she anticipated could see her mood switch to one of high suspicion, with rapid avoidance of anyone coming close and no way to calm her back down again. We had to judge every situation with how things might go if we needed to get her on the lead quickly, as approaching her sharply would result in her jumping and staying out of arm's reach. Constant risk assessment on walks became second nature to me, while all the while staying calm and positive and not wishing to constrain her development and enjoyment of life. She needed to be outdoors, using her senses; it was where she was learning to be herself, a dog living a regular life, not a fecund, money-making object. When she was in the midst of a great long sniff, nose deep in a mound of grass, inhaling, decoding the myriad of odoriferous messages left by previous passersby, she was truly happy. No mistaking her delight in being a dog right then in those moments.

There was no way we were going to deny her the liberty of entering and relishing a world humans cannot perceive. A world of smells and olfactory communication that Twinkle's nose itched to partake of as soon as we left the house. Equally, there was no way we could chance her being without the attached long line to step on in places where we wouldn't be able to take several minutes or longer, if it was needed, to get her back on the lead. Free roaming and sniffing could be achieved with a little help from the trailing line. Things progressed well and we found that so long as we did things in clear, set ways and ensured our behaviour, actions and minds were calm around her, she was an adorable angel while out on walks.

By late autumn, she was at the stage where I felt sufficiently confident with her behaviour in surroundings we were familiar with that I had started to leave off the trailing long line. Then one dank, miserable afternoon I took her and Renae to the local field in between rain showers. Twinkle's aversion to rain is way beyond typical schnauzer dislike of it; at that stage she would become frantic and uncontrollably scared, and once I had seen this we avoided being out in the wet weather if we could. A mortal dread of rain is common in puppy farm dogs and is likely due to the unfamiliarity of the sensation, but also the hosing down of their pens, crates or cages – with them still in. This not only terrorises the trapped dogs, who can't escape the drenching, they can also be injured by these brutal practices, with reports of them losing eyes from being caught by power washers.

I knew we would have to deal with Twinkle's rain phobia in the long term, but avoidance was our safest option at that point. On this particular day all was going well: we had met a couple of dogs and all ran happily together, and Twinkle was her normal self. Then we made to head home and I went to put her on the lead in the usual routine, which consists of me quietly and calmly getting her to sit and saying 'clip', which tells her that my hand reaching round is no threat. This was one of the first things I taught her, and on hearing 'clip' she normally pauses, her head slowly following my hand round, and all is well. Only that day, she was having such fun running with the dogs who were now off across the field that she decided she wanted to join them, bouncing off, tail up, merrily continuing her off-lead playing. It was great to see her happy and as there was no real need to head straight home, I could see no problem letting her and Renae have a little longer. So off we went again round the field, breaking it up with little stop-and-starts for treats, and no lead, so she would not associate the next stop and clip with the end of the walk. This was the first time that I had seen this behaviour in her; all normal, predictable behaviour when puppy training, where resistance to the end of the walk is displayed. It was a revelation to see it in Twinkle that day and although not desirable in normal situations with dogs, I knew it was a sign of progress: she felt confident, happy and able to try a bit of manipulation on me. I made a mental note to adapt our end-of-walk routines to manage this new, confident Twinkle.

But then I spoilt things. It was starting to drizzle and

I was so intent on getting her safely back on the lead that she immediately picked up on my urgency and became uneasy, refusing to sit, or stay within reach. Not good. I tried coaxing her to approach for treats – fortunately I had lots of her favourites with me – but she was having none of it. Coaxing rarely works with Twinkle, even in the calmest of environments; all it does is make her highly mistrustful of what we might be about to do. As the rain fell heavier, I knew I had to stay calm. Not easy as she started to panic, her head rapidly flicking rain drops off and her whole body trembling to the tip of her tail. I bitterly regretted not having the long line attached to her as it was proving impossible to get hold of my scared, confused Twinkle. Almost an hour and many circuits of the field later, circuits involving efforts at distraction, me playing with Renae, anything to get Twinkle's mind to click back into its previously happy state, and nothing was working. A couple of dogs joined us during this time and I was hopeful that the distraction of the dogs – she is always happy to greet dogs – would be enough to snap her out of this alarming mindset. But no, as soon as I approached, off she jumped, edgier than ever.

After a while, it was clear that she was in real turmoil: her tail was tucked, her ears were flat, and she stayed out of arm's reach or moved in the opposite direction if I attempted to approach. She was like a feral dog but not quite, as thankfully she did not actually bolt (small mercies), and came when I called to her. She just refused to stay within reach. How I wished we lived in a place where I could have walked her safely home, allowing her to stay an uneasy few feet away from me, off the lead if she wished. But alas, to get back home we needed to cross several busy roads; there was absolutely no way I could leave the field without her being on the lead.

After an hour, I was pretty worried. I had been trying to stay calm and positive, making it seem like just another walk, albeit one where Twinkle would not allow any approach. I was determined not to stress about the situation we were in, knowing this would scupper any chance of her settling, but it was impossible not to feel rising panic in the ominously gathering evening gloom. Every minute of fading light increased my worries as Twinkle got more worked up. Eventually, I managed to get Michel on the phone and he soon arrived in the car to see if together we could catch her. She was no better with his efforts to entice her to him, despite him being the calmest person on earth; our wild and crazy Twinkle did exactly the same to him, staying out of arm's reach, jumping away if approached. Eventually, between the pair of us we were able to trap her along a narrow footpath. As I walked ahead, Michel walked behind with Renae and Twinkle between us. On my signal, I stopped walking, they stopped and he swiftly grabbed her harness. She fiercely wriggled in his hands, trying to bite, and nearly got away but just in time, after a short scuffle and me grabbing, I picked her up, holding on for dear life. I held her tightly, relief flooding through me. As I cradled her close, her beating heart thumping away below my fingers, mine matching hers, I whispered to myself, to her, "Shush, shush, shush, sweet Twinkle, shush, you are safe, thank god you are safe, sweet girl."

But it was just how I had not wanted it to go, as grabbing and trapping Twinkle could not have helped her emotional state or her confidence at all; it would have been exactly the harsh, hateful actions she'd experienced in her past. But that day, it was the only way to get her safely into our hands and home. I was sorry that we did it, so sorry for Twinkle that the situation had escalated as it had. But she was safe and that was the most important thing.

Then she pulled one of her surprises. Back home, it was like nothing had happened; she seemed completely, wonderfully unperturbed by the drama at dusk. As we walked in the door, Susie-Belle greeted us all, scanning Twinkle from head to toe, and Twinkle behaved as she always does. There was no sign at all that she had just spent the last hour giving me the fright she had, let alone herself. The same could not be said for me. It took a few glasses of wine that evening before I settled down as I reflected on what had happened. I had hoped such alarming behaviour was well and truly behind us but a combination of things had contributed to her frightening response: as the weather had been bad for weeks, and local places were under water or insufferably muddy, we had done fewer off-lead walks and more tedious, pavement walks which I think bored Twinkle, hence her excitement and initial resistance to being put back on the lead. This then coincided with the rain and she panicked, which made me hurry to get her on the lead, which affected her and into the spiral we went. It had all been a horrible escalation of events that I did not want to repeat.

It was another few months before Twinkle was completely free of the trailing long line, as I needed to rebuild my confidence with allowing her full freedom again. But oddly, there has never been any sign again of her acting as she did that afternoon, although she still hates rain. We notched it up to an experience in Twinkle's life journey with us, a constellation of circumstances that in some way, unexpectedly, and inexplicably moved her forwards, frighteningly unwelcome as it was at the time.

> The world breaks everyone and afterward many are strong at the broken places.
>
> – Ernest Hemingway, *A Farewell to Arms*

9

Lunch at the Chateau

To roam the roads of lands remote,
To travel is to live.
– Hans Christian Andersen, *The Fairy Tale of My Life*

During Twinkle's first summer in France, we were invited to stay with our friends Dean and Jolyon who were holidaying a couple of hours away in the Lot-et-Garonne department. We jumped at the invite, for as far as the dogs were concerned we knew they would love a trip to see their best friends. Rupert is close in age to Renae and they have been good pals since puppyhood. With his younger brother Watson, during Susie-Belle's earliest months with us, regularly meeting up with them was a welcome aid in helping her settle into her new life. The healing vibe drawn from the comforting presence of steady, well-behaved dogs for others to whom life has not been so kind is profound; I think it is hard, if not impossible, for humans alone to replicate the unique quality of inter-canine therapy. In her first months with us, we made sure to meet up on a few occasions and Twinkle easily found her place amongst Susie-Belle and Renae's canine friends, readily at ease in their company.

Twinkle has always enjoyed being in the car, sitting up taking everything in as we drive around. For a dog that had lived cooped up in a barren concrete pen, it should not be a surprise that she is keen to see as much as she can of her new surroundings, wherever she is. But she does surprise me, all the time. For she isn't just interested, no – Twinkle, like a sailor in a crow's nest, needs to see everything. Everything. From the moment the car engine starts, she is sitting upright on her bed in the back of the car viewing all she can. Relishing this new dimension to her world, she watches, scans, absorbs and enjoys every moment of drive-time. I melt just a little each time I spy in the rear-view mirror, Twinkle at her lookout, the back of her head moving back and forth, sight-seeing to her heart's content. Often as I try to keep focus on the road ahead, my eyes are drawn to the rear-view mirror, pulled by the simplest of images. One which makes me look again and again to savour the sight, this time of two grey heads, Renae and Twinkle, their synchronised nosiness keeping tabs on the world they watch. While her sisters play lookout, Susie-Belle, I can only assume, lies out of sight snoozing the drive away. Although she has always travelled well, there is a sense with her that a car journey is a bit of a chore, not an adventure. There's no eagerness to sit up, to take her place alongside her sisters watching the world slide past. Susie-Belle, now a seasoned traveller, has decided journeys are made for napping.

So, we readily accepted the invitation, always keen to take a jaunt through the French countryside, knowing Twinkle for one would be happy with the road trip. As we wound our way along quintessentially French, plane-tree lined roads through quiet villages, over rolling hills and a stunning landscape we saw subtle shades of difference in the countryside from that around our house which lies a little farther north. In the Lot we found the shades a little greener, the rows of rich vines more numerous and the valleys deeper. France is a remarkable country for its diverse range of landscapes, each region displaying certain unique characteristics. It is impossible to be bored by such a land and Twinkle sat seemingly mesmerised by the views.

Although we had set off early, as we neared our destination

the heat was already rising and it promised to be a hot day. Keeping the dogs from overheating in their playful excitement would be our priority during the day, our own pleasures taking a firm second place. We had packed their cool pads, frozen treats and iced water along with our swimming costumes, sunscreen and a fat dollop of common sense to manage the heat. Susie-Belle has never been great in high temperatures, but that first summer with us we were astounded by Twinkle's apparent enjoyment of sweltering heat. In the UK, like a sun-worshipping happy lizard, she stayed in our conservatory on the hottest days, despite having free access to other rooms and the garden. We put her favourite bed in the coolest, shadiest places to entice her to leave the stifling heat in the conservatory, but she chose to stay in the warmth, even when her sisters were sensibly snoozing in the shade. As I feverishly fretted about baking dogs in hot places, a friend offered the thought that if I had spent years in a freezing cold concrete pen in a draughty agricultural shed, I may well enjoy the luxuriant warmth of a summer conservatory. True. So I let her be and all seemed easier; she had choices and now chose to be warm.

During our stay with Dean and Jolyon, we had an invitation to lunch nearby. By something of a coincidence, their house lies a couple of miles from that of Sarah and Robbie, owners of Gaspard, a young standard schnauzer. Originally from the UK, Sarah and Robbie now live year-round in France; through social media we'd chatted online for several months and now we had the chance to connect in person. Although I was keen to meet Sarah, Robbie and Gaspard, and I was certain our dogs would be delighted to have a new canine friend to share their day with, there was a further lure for me. They happen to live in a magnificent property, a genuine French chateau dating back to the sixteenth century, and I was almost as eager to have a nosey round the chateau as I was to meet its inhabitants.

We headed out across country on rural back roads and within minutes we were pulling into the long driveway of an impressive piece of Lot architecture. At the end of the sweeping, tree-lined drive stood the chateau complete with turrets and tower.

Sarah hospitably laid on lunch, Robbie being a keen and excellent amateur chef, but before we settled ourselves to spend a pleasurable afternoon in the shade feasting, the dogs needed to run off their excess excitement. Serious exuberance had erupted as soon as Gaspard and his canine brother Diego, a Catalan sheepdog, just a few months old, realised they would be sharing their day with a bunch of foreign invaders, as first Rupert and Watson descended from the car, closely followed by our three. The dogs' excitement was obvious but understandable tensions were rising along with noise levels which pained the ears and it was clear to all that the best thing for tempering the excitable atmosphere was to take a swift, sociable walk. Twinkle, in the midst of what was rapidly escalating into a chaotic doggy meet and greet spiced up by a fair whiff of canine testosterone, was in her element, making quick acquaintance with her male hosts. Diego, nonplussed, left his brother to it, but Gaspard with Gallic charm in abundance was clearly taken with the flirtatious new visiting dog *du jour* who teasingly bounced around under his nose. She was obviously happy, as she had frequently shown herself to be in male doggy company, and with Gaspard the standard schnauzer, Twinkle was saucily intent on making the most of her day out.

After a lot of bottom sniffing, mutual checking out, sizing up and settling down, we eventually headed out to the expansive grounds which lay behind the chateau. We have been on many social dog walks but this was the first in the grounds of a lived-in, bona fide chateau, complete with resident schnauzer. Acres of golden fields of sunflowers lay behind the chateau beyond which the cool distant forest beckoned. Gaspard led the way with his guests close behind, clinging to the shade afforded by the tall sunflowers on the edge of the field. As the dogs wove in and out of the tall plants, Susie-Belle and I brought up the rear as she puffed along, struggling in the heat of the day. Scooping her up, I carried her a good part of the way, thankful when we reached the cool shade of the trees and we could all take a rest. Twinkle and Gaspard lay panting in the cropped grass, tongues flapping, happy in one another's company. Aside from calming the dogs' excitement and moving them into neutral territory, a walk in the heat of an August day had not been the wisest decision. But, after a rejuvenating rest in the welcome protection of the trees, all his guests were keen to follow Gaspard back to the chateau for lunch. Or in my case, lunch and a snoop around.

My inquisitiveness was soon satisfied as Sarah graciously gave us a tour of her impressive home. Living in such a stunning property must bring with it a certain acceptance that visitors might want a tour, but I appreciated Sarah and Robbie's generous tolerance of my ill-disguised nosiness. The thick stone walls of the building cooled the interior of what is a fascinating property. I was suitably awestruck by the sheer size of the place and the amount of work that goes into keeping a chateau feeling homely. For years I had wanted to experience first-hand what life in an authentic French chateau is like, and thanks to the connections made through our dogs I got to do just that. Post-tour, as we relaxed outside on the cool, calm veranda, enjoying good food and beautiful surroundings, Gaspard kept a close eye on his guests. One in particular – in fact there was a definite *affaire d'amour* sizzling with little Twinkle under the table. She was certainly cute with her handsome beau, staying close and playful with him all day. It was wonderful to see her relaxed in a new environment, letting herself forget whatever anxieties usually temper her joyful side. Even a sudden tumble into the ornamental fish pond when one of us unnerved her by moving a chair, and she, naturally, needed to leap out of the way and into the pool, did nothing to dampen her enjoyment of the day. It is reasonable to think a startling plunge into a pond might scare her silly, but once again our assumptions were flawed, for after shaking herself dry, she coolly resumed her place alongside Susie-Belle like nothing had happened.

One of the reasons we have always been keen to network with dogs and their sympathetic humans is to allow Twinkle the chance to feel happy and carefree, even if that lasts only until the next unexpected scare claws her back into the dark den of worry that haunts her. As it is with dogs she so clearly feels happiest, we seek out every occasion to offer her this simple salve, in the hope that each time she moves just a little farther from the darkness that grips her. Our faith in our particular recipe for Twinkle's journey to happiness was again confirmed on the day we spent with Gaspard at the chateau, as for most of it she was happy. Definitely happy.

10

Survival of the Toughest

Nobody realises that some people expend tremendous energy merely to be normal.

– Albert Camus

Twinkle and Susie-Belle suffered at the cruellest end of the commercial breeding spectrum where those with even the smallest of consciences might recognise their confinement as simply animal abuse. But there are places that breed dogs where conditions are not as harsh which are considered by many commercial breeders as adequate: dogs kept in kennels to breed until they have earned their retirement. Even then, there are many that never get to live out their retirements in homes, with families. Many of these commercial breeders will argue that they love their dogs, and giving them beds in their kennels and outside space to run in is completely fine. To me they are all unacceptable – dogs are companion animals and unless they are proper working dogs (and even here, I have doubts) a life in kennels is not good enough. A kennel is still a kennel, not a home with human love and companionship.

Since my first book on puppy farming came out, I have had the privilege of hearing the tales of many dogs with backgrounds which are not as terrible as those endured by Susie-Belle and Twinkle, but which still cause dogs to live deprived, limited lives. They all leave lasting damage, whatever kennel breeders assert to the contrary. Alexa's experience with Daisy and George is typical of many stories shared with me:

> I worked at a boarding kennels that also bred dogs (I was young at the time and only cared about the dogs and did not know any better). They bought in puppies from puppy farms to keep and breed from. They had various breeds including Labradors, Westies, Cavalier Spaniels and shih-tzus. I left the kennels to start college and couldn't bear the thought of poor twelve-year-old George, the ex-stud shih-tzu, dying alone in a cold kennel, and as he had outlived his worth, the kennel owner let me take him home for his retirement. This was much to my parents' despair as we already had two German shepherds.
>
> I thought he would likely only have a few months to live as he was in poor health, but he got much love and lived another five years, deeply loved and cared for by his first ever family. Blind, deaf and tongue hanging out because of all his missing teeth, he moved to France with my parents and was my dad's pride and joy. He carried George everywhere. Finally, George suffered a stroke and left this world, cradled in Dad's arms.
>
> About six months after taking George home, I returned to the kennels to help out during holidays. Daisy, a breeding shih-tzu, had just suffered pyometra and she had to have an emergency spay operation to save her. On her return to the kennels, the owner said in my earshot, "She's no use to me now, she may as well be put down." She was only six years old. She came home with me that evening, even more to my parents' despair. I told them that it was only for the night and she was going back to see her fate the following day, but my dad refused to let her go back.
>
> Poor Daisy had mange, which was passed to her from her mum at the puppy farm and no doubt she

When Twinkle first arrived her place of safety was usually found by staying as close to her sisters as possible, neither of whom ever seemed to mind.

As Susie-Belle's personality and confidence developed, she became an expert in "groking", the art of staring while people are eating in the hope of getting some of their food. (© Kathleen Jaeger)

Twinkle during her first summer never showed any interest in joining me for a swim in the lake but didn't want to be left out, contenting herself with an occasional paddle.

Twinkle, flirting with her new friend, Gaspard, while Renae lay flaked out in the shade under the trees, all closely watched by Rupert.

Domaine de Pradines, the ideal campsite for us, high in the Cevennes mountains, remote, peaceful, well away from the rat-race.

Renae is the perfect sister for Susie-Belle and Twinkle, she's confident, caring and looks out for them, in ways only a dog can do.

*Three sassy schnauzer sisters, happy companions,
enjoying their lives as all dogs deserve to.*

*Pup Aid 2014 was a great day out for us all, when Susie-Belle got
a little tired, a cuddle in my arms soon revived her.*

passed it to all of the puppies she gave birth to. This proved incredibly difficult to get rid of and in the end affected her immunity, and we lost her after several battles with illnesses. But she had reached the grand age of twelve, and flourished in our family, becoming quite a character!

There are times when a little theory chases around in my head, usually triggered by hearing of a dog that survives years of torment and bad health, but who, when rescued, goes on to live a good long life. Dogs that endure nothing but mental and physical abuse in the breeding industry, to the point of death, and yet, when given love and care, thrive. Susie-Belle's years in the puppy farm nearly killed her, yet here she is, one tough little dog, loving life and in not bad health for a senior canine citizen. George had experienced a life of deprivation and poor care, yet he went on to live well into old age. It isn't really my theory, nor unique to breeding dogs, but I see the 'survival of the fittest' in action in many of the survivors, for the ones who experience years of suffering have to be the strong ones. The weak and frail do not last in the brutal environments they are trapped in. Heartbreakingly, however, for the more robust, their very strength and good productivity prolongs their imprisonment. Only when this declines and they are no longer profitable are they released from their torment. The cruel reality is this rarely means rescue and retirement to a peaceful life. No, release from life itself is far more likely to be their fate. Of course, not all who get out to live in kind homes do so in time to restore them to health. There are those who are so worn out, ill or broken that they get to live but a short while in safety and peace before death steals them away. I know there are too many for whom freedom arrives too late.

I had cause to contemplate the robustness of some survivors during Twinkle's second summer stay in France, when she required an emergency trip to the vet. We had arrived the day before after an uneventful night-drive down.

We had opted for an overnight trip as the summer in the UK and across France was a hot delight of endless days of warm sunshine and high temperatures and the dogs would benefit from the cooler night air for their pee-stops. Just before we journeyed, however, Twinkle picked up what we guessed was a slight bug and although she appeared to be fine during the trip, the next morning the household was startled awake with an urgent need for Twinkle to go out and do her business. However, she was as eager as ever to have some breakfast, so before rushing to the vet we decided to see how things developed during the morning and for an hour or so, all was settled. However, in true Twinkle fashion, the dramatics began swiftly and suddenly ramped up so that by mid-morning she had gone from having a loose tummy to passing blood – and lots of it at that. She was drinking great gulps of water which she promptly vomited up, together with more blood. All this within a couple of hours of her seeming to be in fine fettle apart from a touch of softness in her toilet.

Off to the vet we headed *tout de suite*. As we stood on the pavement outside the clinic waiting for it to open after lunch, the epic nature of Twinkle's dramas appeared once again as she squatted for a pee and out poured a stream of fresh blood. As I stood staring at the shocking red puddle pooling on the cobbles, I knew this was fast becoming an emergency. Yet despite all the obvious signs to the contrary, Twinkle really did not appear to be distressed. Stoicism is common to Susie-Belle and Twinkle; they both have tremendous fortitude, no doubt carved from their years of survival.

With the symptoms Twinkle was displaying I guessed there was a good chance the vet would want to admit her for treatment. In preparation for a discussion on this at the clinic, I fretted over the essential nature of the admission being weighed against causing her the additional stress of confinement in a strange environment. For dogs that have lived in small, enclosed spaces, returning to confinement, especially in an unfamiliar setting amongst strangers, can set them back in their rehabilitation, which in Twinkle's case is always fragile. While I knew that admission might be the best clinical option for Twinkle, equally I wanted to be sure that if we agreed to it the staff caring for her were properly aware of her background and unusually high stress response. I had visions of her being matter-of-factly manhandled and biting in fear, or worse to my sensibilities, muzzled, all bringing back terrible memories for her – memories I hope she will never have to relive again. Crazy as it now seems, I worried that if she was admitted she would have no familiarity with the language spoken by those caring for her. It nagged at me: had I or hadn't I read that dogs can distinguish individual words rather than just sounds, so linguistics would matter? Fretting through my memory bank of weird canine facts and half-remembered trivia at least took my worried mind off the troubling truth that she was a seriously poorly dog. Distraction works as well for me as it does most dogs.

While my French conversational skills are enough for me to get by in simple social situations, I rely on Michel as the native speaker to do the talking in any situation beyond the most basic. Much to my frustration, this was going to be a case of me having to concede the task of communicating with the vet, so I needed Michel to be on board with my wish to have Twinkle's background explained, understood and respected. I wanted it clear that of course I would agree to her admission, but only once this had been considerately balanced with her other issues. I had to be involved in any decisions being made on Twinkle's behalf, something that in England is perfectly normal between me and our vet, but in France, because of my failure to learn proficient French, I am forced to relinquish control – not a state I am ever happy in but I have only myself to blame. As we drove to the clinic and I repeated for the umpteenth time to Michel that I had to know what was being discussed and decided between him and the vet, and what the vet needed to be told about Twinkle, I detected a slight roll of Michel's eyes and fleeting whisper of an exasperated sigh.

For years I have been promising him I will improve my French and not for the first time I rued my linguistic laziness.

Aside from the language issues, visiting our local vet here is nothing like our practice in the UK where we see the same wonderful vet most of the time and the nurses are familiar faces who have cared for our companions for many years with compassionate understanding. Our relationship is long-standing, reliable and something I treasure. In order to meet the requirements of the Pet Travel Scheme, we have to go to our French vet each time we return to the UK so we visit several times a year. More visits annually than in England, yet the relationship, which is now many years old, is as different to what we have with our English veterinary team as the French are to the English as a nation. It is a busy practice located in a vibrant market town right in the heart of a stereotypically French rural community with a generous sprinkling of Dutch and British inhabitants. The waiting room reflects the mixed community it serves: florid faces of farmers with their working hounds contrast with the aloof visages of the town's bourgeoisie with their pampered cats and neat poodles. Invariably there will be an interloper, a foreigner who has made France their home or holiday hideaway. Over the years, we have had opportunity to observe this colourful tableau as waiting times are frequently awful. This day, we had arrived at the dreaded turn-up-and-wait afternoon session. This runs for an hour and seems to have no order or pattern to who gets seen first. Names are called in what appears to be a random order. However, the urgency of Twinkle's symptoms and puddle of blood on the cobbles mercifully pushed us to the top of the list and we were called first.

As is often the case, the vet who hurried us into his room was not one we had seen before. Young and a tad brusque, he got straight to the point and immediately focused on Twinkle's symptoms, matter-of-factly taking her temperature before I had time to blurt out my basic *elle a peur des être humains*: she fears people. As he firmly inspected ears, eyes and mouth

100

– all completely terrifying touches to Twinkle whose skin at that time, eighteen months on from being out of the puppy farm, would still reflexively ripple if unwanted or unexpected touch happened – I tried to show the need to handle her gently by stiffening my spine and standing straighter as he pulled her back end towards him and I stroked her beard. I caressed her ears with a frustrated, half-suppressed tut, trying to stay calm and not add to her stress by showing my dismay at the tersely efficient examination. I tried subtly using my body language to bring this busy, focused professional's attention to what Michel was telling him regarding Twinkle – our special, sensitive, petrified girl – not only her symptoms. I huffed and puffed and attempted to make him slow down with the examination. He soon did. After the snippy start, with the air filling with my soft, barely concealed sighs and Twinkle's racing heart being heard, Michel's words began filtering through and this clinical professional softened his manner, giving Twinkle's rump a gentle rub of Gallic affection before beginning the many injections he said were needed.

It is unfair of me to be irritated by an efficient, knowledgeable professional doing the job expected; faced with a dog with the symptoms we described, that is what his focus was and of course, should have been. But what the whole episode showed me again was how hard it is at times for Twinkle to function in the world of humans. There we were, all there to help her, but she could not possibly grasp this as she was manhandled, prodded, poked and jabbed. And because strokes and cuddles do not reassure her, normal displays of affection we rely on to comfort our dogs are of limited use to Twinkle. But I did it anyway, holding her while the vet gave his injections – which seemed to go on forever – and massaging her trembling ears, whispering softly to her that it was going to be just fine, that she was going to get better with our help, she just needed to do that hardest of things, trust us.

It was decided mutually that as she was so stressed

treatment at home for twenty-four hours was the best option, but if it did not take effect by the morning, or she worsened at all, then she would be admitted. The vet, to give him full credit, did not need me to tell him this was the right course of action – he recognised her stress when his stethoscope touched her chest. Heaven knows what her heart rate was. I hope that he also heard Michel's words explaining just what our funny, special, peculiar Twinkle has been through in her life and why examinations are even more traumatic for her than most dogs.

Thankfully the treatment worked – the vet entirely knew what he was doing. His diagnosis and treatment of a severe case of haemorrhagic gastroenteritis combined with a urinary tract infection – typical Twinkle to have both at the same time – was spot on. Not that I ever doubted he'd get it right. I just needed him to recognise the individual dog on his table, not merely a set of symptoms. With characteristic rapidity (anything with Twinkle can change in a flash), within twenty-four hours she was well on the road to being back to her normal self. Whatever normal is.

> If you are always trying to be normal, you will never know how amazing you can be.
>
> – Maya Angelou

11

Lola's Legacy

Courage and perseverance have a magical talisman,
before which difficulties disappear and obstacles
vanish into air.

– John Quincy Adams

While I think dogs that endure years and survive long enough eventually to escape the breeding machinery of the puppy business are the stronger ones, their puppies frequently are not. Reports abound of puppies being bought only to fall ill shortly afterwards. Campaigners and investigators can all tell an extraordinarily dismal number of individual stories of suffering puppies. Numerous readers of *Saving Susie-Belle* contact me to share their experiences, many just heartbreaking.

The people buying the poorly puppies are left often feeling bitter both at their own bad experiences, but above all that, bitterness on behalf of the canine babies they watched struggle for life. Struggles which are often lost. Others speak, full of understandable anger, while many feel guilt at being part of the filthy trade, guilt they find hard to shake even when puppy buys are researched, not casual, naive or mindless. One thing they all share with me is a dedication to do what they can to stop other dogs and puppies suffering.

Many of the puppies that are bred badly are already ill when they are traded, sold and bought. Too often many never recover, or if they do it can cost their new owners a small fortune in veterinary fees to help them pull through. While some first-time puppy buyers are duped through naivety or lack of experience, even those who might know better can be taken in by sly dealers and breeders using all the tricks of their dirty trade to fool buyers they sell puppies to. Rebecca recounts her experience:

My partner and I were looking to get another Labrador; he had tons of experience with dogs and actually worked them but they were also our pets. We were looking for a gundog. We came across an attractive advertisement from a breeder and went to see him. He showed us Dad (it wasn't Dad) and Mum, but she wasn't in with the puppy (looking back I don't think she was Mum either). As well as the Labradors he had other breeds for sale and all dogs were sectioned off. With hindsight we were taken in by the breeder's confidence and pitch; we were gullible and did not do our homework on him. We purchased our gorgeous black Lab on our second visit.

Muddy was ill from the beginning with severe diarrhoea. We phoned the breeder, who first made dietary suggestions and said it was normal and down to the transition. After several heated discussions – the man was a bully – our calls were ignored. Things for Muddy deteriorated; she was opened up at the vet's and she had intestinal abnormalities but was not tested for parvo virus. She was put to sleep in her second week with us. It was devastating. We loved her like she had been with us a lifetime.

Lots of investigations were done and it was concluded that she had suffered every symptom of the parvo virus. We discovered that the breeder traded under several names. We involved every agency we could and eventually he was prosecuted and fined for breeding and selling dogs without a licence. It turned out that he had knowingly sold dogs with parvo on many occasions. The man is pure evil when it comes to animal welfare; he could not have cared less that he was selling sick puppies.

Rebecca's experience is far from rare and with the easy, often anonymous advertising of puppies offered by Internet selling, dealers of factory-farmed puppies have access to high volumes of potential buyers in ways not seen in the past. Once bought, if puppies fall ill it is not uncommon for buyers to be unable to contact the person they bought the puppy from – they simply disappear. This is one major risk of buying a puppy from anywhere other than the breeder's home.

With the atrocious conditions commonly found in puppy farms and bad commercial breeding kennels, it is unsurprising that many puppies suffer like Muddy did, and sadly succumb to infectious diseases like parvo virus. Their lives are short and miserable, their tiny bodies racked by any number of problems. Yet once the money is handed over, the dealers are unlikely to spare them another thought. The callous cycle of canine suffering for easy profit continues unchecked all the while there is demand from puppy buyers. But it is not just infectious diseases that puppies coming from abusive breeding environments are prone to – genetic problems are rife and terrible. In the US, the story of one puppy, Lola, has inspired many people to take action against puppy mills. Her story is best told by her adopter, Sandra:

Lola was saved from a puppy mill at the age of seven weeks. She was discarded because she was born with only one eye. A national rescue saved her and she went immediately into foster care with pneumonia. A few weeks later I met this little showgirl and she pranced her way into my heart. I adopted her, but after a few months she started walking in circles. It seemed more than the typical circular activity when excited. I took her to the veterinarian and they said it was serious. We took her to a specialist who tested her and determined that she had necrotizing meningoencephalitis, a genetic disorder that had caused huge damage throughout her brain. It is a dreadful disease and I was told that it was terminal. At the age of six months old she had a death sentence, likely due to inbreeding. She started having convulsions that wouldn't stop and she died in my arms with the help of our vet. Before she died, she had won the hearts of many via social media. They grieved with me and we all united in a cause: to regulate these puppy mills. She is survived by a canine 'brother', Luka, who has taken up the mantle for the cause. Her name was Lola, she was a showgirl.

If there is anything positive that can be said to have come from the needless suffering and early death of Lola, it is that her tragic story triggered a powerful response from many thousands of campaigners in the United States. Her legacy is a powerful one and largely through social media her family and thousands of supporters continue to fight a strong campaign to bring an end to the suffering of dogs in puppy mills. Every year, on her birthday in October, and on the day of her death, April 15th, supporters send letters to lawmakers, legislators, both local and national, and to the US president, pleading to regulate puppy mills. They send their missives in bright pink envelopes, a fitting tribute to Lola.

> And she sits and gazes at me
> With those deep and tender eyes,
> Like the stars, so still and saint-like,
> Looking downward from the skies.
> – Henry Wadsworth Longfellow, *Footsteps of Angels*

In a way, the puppies that are born with obvious issues and get out of the puppy farms early are the fortunate ones, as with luck, they find their way into homes where the right care is given and they can live well. Puppies at least have their spirits intact and if removed early enough can put their dreadful beginnings behind them. Tracey, a veterinary nurse, has much experience of caring for dogs and puppies that are taken into rescue from time to time from a puppy farm located close to the practice where she works. She shared her thoughts with me on the difficult role played by the rescuers and the tightrope they must walk in their relationships with the puppy farmers:

> The process of collecting the 'reject' puppies, the 'faulty' ones, must involve a lot of restraint on behalf of the rescue. The relationship between puppy farmer and dog rescue is complex. The rescuers know their hands are pretty much tied for if they break the chain and stop taking the 'used up stock', the damaged and ill, what will happen to those poor dogs? They know they just have to commit to picking up the pieces and trying to undo the damage caused to these animals. Last year a tiny pure-bred puppy that was failing to thrive was placed in a plastic container by the puppy farmer in the hope that it would pass away overnight. However, he survived the night and the following day he was in the care of the rescue. Sadly, despite all the treatment possible being given, he did not survive, but his remaining days were spent being loved and properly cared for.
>
> You can almost plot the timelines of these poor dogs. Many of the puppies are born with a natural resilience and zest for life; the world to them is exciting and new (even though very restricted). It is as they start to mature that the rot sets in and you can see many of them becoming highly fearful, some almost feral in behaviour. I know several that left the puppy farm when they were about a year old. No dog should be as scared of the world around them as they are. One thing

I will add, however, and that is the same for almost all the puppy farm dogs that I have encountered, the fear that they show rarely develops into aggression, which always amazes me. Personally I wouldn't blame them for displaying aggression towards people. As these dogs approach middle age many just seem to give up, their spirits are well and truly broken and they just seem empty.

The work of rescuers is thankless and never ending. While most are entirely focused on saving the dogs, sadly there are some which are seen to cross the line between rescue work and becoming a profitable link in the puppy trade. Unfortunately this means that other honest, genuine rescues receive criticism from those who view them as complicit in the puppy farming industry. The issues are complex, as without the rescues those who are courageously doing the tough work – non-profitably and from a charitable stance, persevering daily to make a difference – the dogs would be disposed of by the puppy farmers and more suffering will result. Puppy farmers are going to get rid of their used up stock one way or another and the cheaper the better.

In her veterinary practice Tracey sees close up on a regular basis just what her local rescuers deal with:

> We now expect in the early part of each year to receive a large influx of ex-breeding stock, what we cynically refer to as 'stock clearance'. I strongly suspect that these dogs are no longer profitable as litter sizes tend to drop as the dogs age (I also imagine that many bitches will start to resorb litters). Another interesting observation is that despite the fact that in some puppy farms the breeding is totally without planning or structure – that is, the stud dogs are just left with the breeding bitches – there have been very few that have come into rescue that are pregnant. Again, due to the small litter sizes in some

of these dogs, we have started to pregnancy scan them as they come in. If the bitches are visibly pregnant when the rescuers go in to collect them, they will be held back by the puppy farmers, but it can be difficult to tell without scanning as some of the breeding bitches can be quite round and odd-shaped and can easily hide a pregnancy with a small litter size. A little dog slipped through the net late last year and produced two puppies not long after being collected – a small victory over the puppy farmers, who would be kicking themselves if they knew.

My job is to help these poor dogs on their journeys back to health. When there are large intakes, one of our vets will go straight to the rescue to pregnancy scan the bitches and start to formulate treatment plans. Most of the long-haired dogs are badly matted, especially around their rear ends, so initial emergency clipping is usually the starting point. I have done some emergency grooming and the audible 'thunk' of a wad of matted fur containing dried faeces and soaked with urine hitting the floor when it was removed sounded like someone had dropped a brick. Yet these poor dogs live with that for years.

We see all sorts with the dogs: rotten, infected mouths, ears full to the brim with wax and filth, tumours, hernias (both umbilical and inguinal), eyes affected by glaucoma that are excruciatingly painful, cataracts – the list is endless, and yet these dogs display little or no pain at all; they have crossed that point and are well beyond it.

Nursing these dogs is a total challenge; most have to be carried everywhere as they cannot and will not walk on a lead when they are first brought into rescue. They give nothing away at all; we know they must be terrified to be in a new and busy environment but they do not react. They settle well in their kennels (maybe feeling the security of an enclosed space) and many shun their comfy bedding, moving it aside and lying on the kennel floor. Heat control for them is challenging as they struggle to cope with the normal ambient temperatures of a vet's kennel room. We tend to switch the lights off and leave them alone, which is really hard for nurses to comprehend and to deal with but the less is more approach is always the best way forward.

In Tracey's account I recognise much of what Susie-Belle and Twinkle both brought with them when they arrived in our lives. Susie-Belle took a long time to relax on a soft bed; she simply did not seem to recognise that comforts are good. She would sit with her shoulders slumping, head hanging, then just as she looked like she was about to drift off and lay down, she would pull herself back and sit stiffly upright, not allowing herself to relax. It was months before this changed. Nowadays that is a thing of the distant past as she takes up the centre of the many soft dog beds that are scattered around the house. Out of our three dogs she is always the first and the most eager to plop herself contentedly down, surrounded by soft cushions, making up for all those lost years.

Tracey mentions heat regulation. We have often wondered at this, as Susie-Belle dramatically pants as soon as the temperature begins to climb and she is way ahead of both Renae and Twinkle at cooling herself down. Twinkle does the same dramatic panting, but seems to enjoy being warm. Hearing that this is a common response in the vet clinic, I wonder if it is a combination of the part of the brain that regulates temperature control being damaged in utero, combined with a behavioural response: they know just how dreadful they may soon feel if they overheat or get too cold, living in conditions where both extremes occur and there is no escape, so they ratchet up their temperature-coping behaviour as soon as they detect there is a need to. It is only my amateur speculation, but it makes sense to me that anything is possible with the dogs as they have to cope with whatever conditions they are trapped in, and their coping behaviour will never leave them, however comfortable their lives subsequently become. Survival instincts are strong in the dogs that get out.

Tracey's insights are disturbing and shocking and I would like all puppy buyers to be forced to see this side of the puppy industry. Is that too mean of me to wish this on someone choosing a cute little puppy to join their family? Too bad if some do think I am mean. The parent dogs are far from cute as they are forced to sit in their own filth. The reality is there. It is often hidden, but when it is actually exposed and in the public domain it is wilfully ignored by many. If people really did share a day with Tracey, a 'stock clearance day', and saw what she and others like her do in their work, would that change their mind about buying a cheap puppy? If they held the trembling bodies of the traumatised, sick, suffering parents of the sweet puppy they are about to buy, smell their rotten mouths and infected wounds, would that stop them buying the puppy in the pet shop, or from the puppy website, or at the local garden centre? Surely something must awaken people for this nightmare for the dogs to end.

12

Up a Mountain with Vultures

*We are all visitors to this time, this place. We are just
passing through. Our purpose here is to observe, to
learn, to grow, to love and then we return home.*
– Australian Aboriginal proverb

Up until four years ago I had never camped in my life. Never
wanted to. The supposed joys of living outdoors in a tiny
space with no home comforts to soften the ordeal held no
appeal. Despite years of Michel trying to persuade me that it
would be a lot of fun and really was something we should do
each summer, I held out against his efforts to convince me to
pitch a tent.

Then along came Susie-Belle and our world changed,
and with it my attitude to camping. In her first year with us,
and ever since, we've been determined to show her and now
Twinkle too, that life outside the puppy farm is full of new
adventures and fun. Friends suggested camping with dogs is
a lot of the latter and they were right. We took it up as a hobby
to help Susie-Belle and it has helped us all: Michel finally gets
to sleep under canvas and relive happy memories of his youth
spent camping out under the stars on Mediterranean beaches;
the dogs get us sleeping at ground level with them; and I have
put aside my reservations and prejudices as I've seen that in
short bursts, camping can indeed be quite a giggle. All this,
despite most of our camping experiences being rain-soaked,

chilly weekends in true British camping tradition.

In Twinkle's first summer we decided that as we would be in France for several weeks, we may as well extend our camping repertoire away from the wet British summer and head to the south of France for what would be for us, a novel experience: a camping trip under blue, not black, skies. It would also be a chance to enjoy swimming in different rivers or lakes, a hobby that I enjoy, Michel occasionally joins me in when the air and water temperatures push the mercury suitably high, and one that Susie-Belle loves to do with me. Twinkle has yet to show any interest, let alone willingness to join in wild swimming and we abandoned hopes of Renae ever doing it after her first summer and clear aversion to it. From her being a puppy I have hankered after sharing my summer swims with Renae, tried my hardest to encourage her into rivers, lakes and seas, but all to no avail. Her abundant dislike of the wet stuff, and bewilderment at why anyone would think she would want to get her paws wet, was as clear as the crystal waters of our local French river we spend hot afternoons visiting. I admit to it taking me a while to leave her be and to respect her wishes to be a dry-land dog. Susie-Belle on the other hand swims like an otter, and is happy to follow me into the waters wherever we are. I am indebted to my perfectly accommodating Susie-Belle for letting me have at least one swimming schnauzer to share my hobby with. And before you think it, I am already there: I know I should be living with spaniels or Labradors.

Looking for a suitable campsite that was within reasonable travelling distance of our house in southwest France proved harder than I had imagined. Our requirements seemed simple: a site that took dogs, wasn't particularly large or busy, and was near some swimmable body of water, preferably a lake. That was it; we could live with most variations so long as these were met. The coast was out of the question as in August French seaside campsites are packed to the gunnels with families; noisy, hectic places with tents crammed closely together, the epitome of a holiday hell for our little pack of canines (and us) as we all crave the peace and quiet – and never more so than when pitching a tent.

After hours of searching online, reading reviews, pondering a few possibilities and discarding many for being too far, too large, too small, dog-unfriendly, too child-friendly, miles from water of any sort, or just too much bother, I finally found what looked like the perfect place for us, Domaine de Pradines. Located high in the mountains of the Cévennes National Park, the campsite promotional pitch promised to show us 'the pleasures of true camping in a vast natural landscape. Each will be able savour the pleasure of a true holiday, in calm surroundings, large spaces, freedom... Set away from the roads, fifty pitches are dispersed between two pine woods, as well as a large open field.'

The alluring blurb convincingly continued to draw me southeast over the Massif Central to the other side of France, in fact much farther than we had initially planned on travelling, the Domaine de Pradines being an ancient Templar site, which 'is a unique site for those seeking space, nature and spectacular landscapes. A corner of paradise to discover.'

As well as fitting the bill for uncluttered camping away from the crowds, a big attraction of the site for me was its proximity to the region's main river, the Tarn. I have long studied the most appealing rivers in France for swimming with the dreamy hope of dipping into many over time and the Tarn comes close to the top of my to-swim list. Everything I have read says this river is one of France's most exquisite, with its turquoise water cutting through wild breathtaking scenery. Several years ago, Michel and I drove through the stunning Gorges du Tarn, and promised ourselves we would revisit; it is too grand a landscape to savour only once. Although we knew the Tarn, neither of us were familiar with the Cévennes region, it not being a well-visited corner of France; people tend to pass through it on their way south to the more popular coastal hotspots. All of which put it firmly in our favour: sparsely populated, wild landscapes, vast open spaced campsite, low-key facilities, gorges, rivers, perfect. And vultures. Not that we hoped to see any of these magnificent birds, although spotting a scene more typical of Africa would be fun. To be in a place where vultures are found certainly sounded remote and peaceful enough to satisfy us. There was just one slight niggle in my mind which I kept quiet about and hoped Michel wouldn't mention: I hate mountain driving.

A few years ago, we spent a memorable holiday staying with a friend who lives high in the Alpes-de-Haute-Provence. This region has truly amazing scenery, and we spent days exploring the fantastic Gorges du Verdon and stunning mountain towns, like Moustiers-Sainte-Marie, Castellane and Entrevaux. It is a fabulous part of France, but the sheer cliffs and dramatic drops off the edges of twisting mountain roads really did play havoc with my terrible acrophobia and I have struggled to drive on roads with even a modest climb ever since. Being a passenger is worse, for driver and me, as I fear the whole time we are about to take a tumble over the side. It is not a good state of mind to be in or spend time around. Pity the driver, pity the passenger. Avoidance is best. So opting to head off from the soft rolling landscape of Périgord where we normally hang out in France to the mountains of the Cévennes was a peculiar decision. I put it down to the irresistible allure of the ideal, sparse-looking campsite and the chance to swim the Tarn. As we packed the car and began the long drive south and east, I hoped I would cope with the climb into the mountains.

As it turned out, the region was a lot less mountainous than I had feared; the climbs were gentler, although they reached great heights, and the roads were more amenable to an acrophobic driver with far less traffic hurtling along them than in the busier Alpine region. In fact throughout our stay we often drove miles without seeing another car. The blissful sparsity of humans and their vehicles we truly felt blessed to find. No less so than because this was the height of summer,

August, when most of France holidays. Thankfully not in the Cévennes. There were a few moments where roads got a little too narrow and drops over the edge were a touch too close and sheer for comfort, but it was all manageable with only an occasional mild panic from me.

Speaking of panic, at that time Twinkle was still on a high level of alert most days, maddeningly skittish on others and prone to dramatic reactions if things weren't as she expected. But as with Susie-Belle, camping helps Twinkle: something about being outdoors, in relaxed company, in close proximity to us, literally sharing the space together, seems to soothe Twinkle's nerves. As we drove around the region, searching out good spots to spend the days, Twinkle was in her element, sat up in her bed for the ride of her lifetime, seeing the world as she had never seen it before. Watching her enjoying the ride, each day blossoming a tiny bit more as she set her fears aside, made us really, simply, happy.

I have often reflected that my complete and utter fear of heights, which cripples me when it hits, must be how she feels a lot of the time when terror takes over. Just as I cannot function or move a muscle, or talk myself to a point of calm, or hear those around me telling me I am safe and there is nothing to fear, this must be how she feels. Overwhelmed. Incapable of response. No amount of reassuring me helps when I'm tipped over the edge. Not literally of course, although the terror I feel is as real as that happening. I cannot think, act or behave normally. Yet most of the time I am a normal human being. Or so I am told.

It has helped me to understand that for Twinkle, at the times that she has been far off the scale of being able to cope with what is terrifying her, no amount of reassurance from us can be understood. It simply will not filter through the engulfing blind terror. Although it makes us feel better to whisper honeyed, soothing words, it does not help Twinkle, although we do it anyway. When I am in the grip of a height-fearing, stiffened-with-terror state, where lifting even just my eyes to see I am safe is impossible as my body rigidly fixes itself to the mast of paralysing acrophobia, nothing and nobody can help me. Just as I need to get away from the edge, or down to level ground, or off the escalator, or down from the bridge to let my irrational responses and mad fear dissipate, so Twinkle needs to be given time and space to bring herself back to relative calm, and given help to avoid whatever triggers the fear in her. A gung-ho approach to making her face her fears, pushing her through, or immersing her in what is terrifying will never help, just as putting me near the edge has never helped me. My acrophobia is best left unstirred by complete avoidance, and this is similar to how I believe Twinkle is best helped. Others may disagree, other dogs will be different, but for us, it is how we are travelling this journey of life together, Twinkle and I. On this level, I get her.

The Cévennes region was exactly what we had hoped to find: a combination of vast open plateaus, the Causses and steep valleys, rich forests, hamlets and villages with ancient quirky buildings clinging to cliffs and hillsides, isolated farms and rivers perfect for swimming. The Tarn lived up to every high expectation I had of it, and we found several places to sample its truly turquoise waters. We could not have found a more idyllic place for the week. We explored the region by car and on foot, following poorly marked trails and scrambling up rough, rocky footpaths to discover secret pools with mountain-fresh glacial waterfalls which we spent hot afternoons splashing in. We were watched over by the dogs, who were all immune to the refreshing appeal of cool swims in mountain rivers and rocky pools. Even Susie-Belle was reluctant, although that was likely due to her being a bit out of sorts.

The day we arrived and set up camp, I noticed a hard red swelling on her bottom under her tail. She let me examine it, but when I lightly pressed it, she frantically wriggled and squealed, a sound rarely heard from her. One thing with Susie-Belle that is never in doubt is how fully she complies with anything we need to do. I have always been thankful for this with her, as she has had to have daily eye care and several other awkward examinations. To imagine applying cream into Twinkle's eyes, I am pretty certain it would not be done with the same quiet compliance that Susie-Belle allows. While I am grateful for her tolerance, it also brings sadness to think how her abusers would have had it easy; there would have been no chasing round trying to catch Susie-Belle in the puppy farm. The poor dog would have just hunkered down and put up with whatever misery was coming her way. Inspecting the lump, I suspected she may have either been stung by something, or, and this I hoped was not the case, she had an abscess, which I know are excruciatingly painful. Not at all what Susie-Belle needed just as we set up camp several miles from the local village and veterinary clinic. We bathed it as well as we could with an antiseptic wash, gave her one of her painkillers and hoped for the best that night.

We woke early in the morning to Susie-Belle fidgeting about in the tent and an almighty mess. What had clearly been a developing abscess had burst and a sticky mixture of bloody pus was being spread over the bedding and her sisters as Susie-Belle tried to get herself comfortable. Being up a mountain at a remote campsite, while utterly beautiful and perfect in all ways, seemed less than ideal right then. We needed to find a vet or pharmacy and seek help for Susie-Belle's tender bottom. And clear up the mess. Pharmacies in France are different to those in the UK. They often have a terrific range of herbal and homeopathic preparations, as well as masses of pharmaceuticals. Even the tiniest village will have a well-stocked pharmacy, probably several, and the staff are usually founts of knowledge. We headed to the nearest town, which was miles away, and decided first to seek advice in a pharmacy seeing as Susie-Belle did not seem unwell, having scoffed a hearty breakfast and come looking for more.

True to form, the pharmacist was as helpful as we have come to expect from French pharmacists over the years and we left with a treasure chest of antiseptic washes and salves to help Susie-Belle's bottom once again be beautiful and pain-free. Within a day or so of us bathing, salving and hoping, healing was well underway. Speaking back home with Janet, who as well as being Susie-Belle and Twinkle's foster mum is also a qualified veterinary nurse, she told me if it had indeed been an anal abscess, which sounds likely, Susie-Belle must have been in excruciating pain. Her years of unbearable pain in the puppy farm have left her with a stoicism which is both a blessing and a curse, for if she had shown us any distress, we would have found a veterinary clinic without hesitation and got her proper pain relief. But seeing as she seemed fine in herself, and the deluge of pharmaceuticals worked so quickly, we thought we were doing the best thing. Maybe we did. She certainly had no recurrence and enjoyed her days camping and watching us swim, albeit without her.

A final remarkable epilogue to this memorable trip to the Cévennes was when months later Janet happened to mention friends with a house in the mountains somewhere remote in France. On further discovery, it appeared that a photograph we had taken of us swimming in the Tarn, in a quiet, quite isolated village, with a house in the background, is the house of Janet's great friends who live there during the spring and summer each year. Of all coincidences, this was one that had us stumped: not only had we chosen to visit one of the remoter areas of France, we then swam in a river in a remote village, at the end of the garden of a house which is inhabited by Susie-Belle and Twinkle's foster mum's friends, who she has known for many years and who have loved and owned schnauzers themselves for years! Of all places for us to stop and swim that day.

Everything in the universe has a rhythm, everything dances.

– Maya Angelou

13

Me, the Muddler

Pardon my sanity in a world insane.

– Emily Dickinson

When Susie-Belle first came into our lives, I had no idea how deeply affecting I would find her presence or where the journey with her would take us all. As she healed and grew into the quite normal, if extraordinary dog she is, I found myself undergoing a transformation that is still underway. The addition of Twinkle, with all her problems, sped up the change in me, from being someone aware of animal suffering to one looking out for it, attempting to do something to stop it. This creates plenty of frustrations and difficulties as I can no longer ignore or tolerate what I may once have. Unreservedly loving two dogs who are the living expression of damage done by the puppy farming industry, yet knowing they are just two of many millions, it can all feel just too overwhelming some days and a deep pit of despair threatens to pull me in. But I plough on, my contributions seeming paltry against what is a daily tsunami of suffering. As I write and try to educate, using whatever means I have to act, to do something, I tell myself a difference is being made; somewhere, someone is being reached and a change is happening. I start each day knowing the dogs cannot liberate themselves from the nightmare, and I have to play my part, big or small, in doing it for them.

When I cannot act, I read. A lot. Good stories and bad. Bad are easy to come across, there being so many. News stories that inspire hope, and those that dash it. Books, papers, journals, all showing dogs to be more amazing than once thought possible, with a psychological sophistication that astounds. I love this. I rejoice that dogs are now being shown to have brilliantly inventive minds, brains that operate in ways astonishingly similar to ours. They think, learn and problem-solve in remarkably effective ways; they feel empathy, can reason, they know when they are being lied to. Only, my celebration of their sophistication is tempered by the hard realisation that their suffering at the hands of humans is then even more dreadful. Just for a second, put yourself in the place of Twinkle, cooped up in a barren concrete pen for years, hungry, cold, terrified and confused. Or imagine for a moment one of her puppies, just one bewildered, terrified infant mind, capable of tremendous thought processes; his tiny, vulnerable body crammed into a crate, in a dark van, on a long, noisy, terrifying journey to the pet shop, to be gawped at, picked up, prodded, then left alone in the dark shop when it closes, to wonder what has happened to him; to cry for his mother, to fear what happens next. Horrible to think about. Remember dogs' brains are similar to ours, so whatever we imagine is close to what they experience. Dumb animals they are not.

I find, read and exult over plenty of fun stuff too – if I didn't, my equilibrium would be done for, and that way an unsound mind lies. That is not going to happen, for without a reasonably level-headed me – if that indeed is what I am – to guide her, how will Twinkle, my wild, crazy, marvellous Twinkle, ever learn just how happy she can be? She needs me and I need her to help keep me on the path that Susie-Belle first set me out on. When sad realities and horrific truths threaten to overwhelm, I take a refreshing, time-wasting rollick around the silly pages on social media, of which there are millions. Dogs doing cute things, dogs being daft, dogs loving life... A few minutes revelling in this and I am soon recharged. Not always enough to resume my research into the gut-wrenchingly awful end of the dog breeding business, but sufficient to know I can keep doing my bit, bringing the end a little closer. I hope.

Then, when I feel like delving deeper, testing the icy waters of the despair pit to see how deep I dare venture, I dip into reading dark academic papers on what makes individuals abuse animals. I can never spend too long there, grappling to understand how the humans who harm them cannot see dogs as I, and others, do: creatures like us, with emotions, with enormous capacity to love and be hurt. I find myself reading through half-closed eyes, holding my breath; like watching a gory horror film with a cushion to my face, peeping round its edges, I skim over details, not wanting to risk giving the awfulness too much of my mind.

I read studies that challenge the stereotype of the 'sick monster' who harms animals; that it is only some other type of person who can do the harm that fills pages on social media and newspapers and my mind. The type that crams the vans with puppies and transports these terrified babies across Europe or the US; the ones who keep parent dogs in the dark for years on end and turn them over to others to pick up the pieces, in the pitiful states described by Tracey. The type of person who sells petrified, sick, injured dogs in auctions, along with the wire cages they will spend their entire lives in. If they are 'sick' does this make them unaccountable for their actions? Are they not responsible? When Susie-Belle left the puppy farm, emaciated, suffering painful infections, rotten teeth and unimaginable terror, was the person who did that to her a monster who knew no better? In some ways, it might be easier to think they were. But no, they were – are – in business, making money from her suffering. Simple. They made the money. Easy money. To them, the abuse was personally beneficial. This I now know – thanks to researchers doing what I could never do, getting in close to those who harm and looking into their minds – is a characteristic common to animal abusers. To me, puppy farming is animal abuse given another name. It is also said that animal abuse results from ignorance of the consequences to the animals. Well how money blinds.

Puppy farmers will often declare a love for their animals when challenged. They are not all quite how we may choose to imagine these 'monsters', those 'others' who keep this industry churning out the goods. These are the ones who begin their breeding business from a position of genuinely loving their dogs, but rapidly see the easy money that can be made, so they soon scale up and with it, the love of money takes over from any love for their dogs. Dogs who are, in effect, pimped, so the owners, aka breeders, can live off the earnings they make from their confinement – and abuse. But all the while, the puppy farmer believes and cries out to all who object, challenge or accuse that they really, really do love their dogs and their dogs love them. An account from a rescuer, who I'll keep anonymous, is particularly disturbing:

> I have to say one of the most shocking facts to me is the profile of a puppy farmer [...] older women, almost grandmotherly types. And the dichotomy of the emotional tears at handing over their 'babies' versus the horribly mistreated and unhealthy dogs they hand over. Their tears appear genuine. It's difficult wrapping my head around understanding how exactly they think they are treating their 'babies'. Very odd.

On rare occasions when I'm researching, where I slip, let go and sink too far into the scummy grim pit trying to understand what I will never fully manage to, I give in to the fierce rage I feel against those who harmed Susie-Belle and Twinkle and millions of others. I scream at the injustice, the falsities, beliefs, traditions and plain old-fashioned lies that are used to justify keeping dogs in hell so that money can be made from them. I rail at the endless social and political factors that we must all tackle to stop the catastrophe for dogs that mankind is inflicting, for profit and that alone. Tears of anger, frustration and sadness blur words and I can read or write no more as my heart aches for the dogs who are our unique companions. Like no other species they have co-evolved over thousands of years, being shaped for lives that millions trapped in breeding places around the world will never get to live. What a shocking barbarism that is.

At times when my equilibrium gets lost, I feel apoplectic at society's apparent lack of willingness to stop it. Read any story of animal abuse or abandonment and people are quick to comment, to label those responsible as 'monsters', usually followed by a string of imaginative ways in which they would like to make them suffer in return. And yet when it comes to buying their puppies, these monsters are finding easy buyers; there is a thriving modern market in cuteness. Without the behaviour of the puppy-buying public supporting the vast scale of commercial puppy breeding, where millions of puppies are bred and sold around the world each year, the business would not be viable. While those running the breeding operations, dealing in and selling the puppies are pilloried and hated by those who see it as plain and simple animal abuse, millions of puppy buyers are letting them off the hook and keeping them in business. Each day I wonder exactly what it will take to change this.

Then the apoplexy passes, the scattered angry thoughts settle back in place, clearing the way for calmer processing of information, and on I go to write and fight another day. To try to make a difference and not go mad with rage at it all. I count the moments of calm with Twinkle, the close times we spend together these days as her confidence grows and her personality strengthens. I look into her eyes and see that where she once never knew what being companionable was, what being calm could be like, now she does, slowly, certainly not all the time, but it is there and it is gaining strength. The bonds with us are firm and each day is better than ever. Musing on Twinkle keeps me going, stops my mind from shattering with the dreadfulness of what puppy farming continues to be around the world for other dogs like her who will never know what she now does.

I read somewhere that once sufficient numbers of people in society experience enough moral shocks, things will change. This hope keeps me from despondency when I see the suffering, but others appear blinded to it as they buy their puppy online or in a pet shop and claim not to know about puppy farms. Can the ignorance really be that great with information everywhere? It seems so. My moral shocks over the past few years have been deep, troubling and numerous, and from them a surge of impatience, of needing to act quickly for dogs like Susie-Belle and Twinkle, has swept away any prior passive interest. So I join others who are way ahead of me on this path by creating a few moral shocks each day if that is what is needed. I talk a lot, write more, share information, challenge what I may once have let go, and keep going and going, hoping it makes a difference.

The philosopher and animal advocate Tom Regan describes three types of animal advocates: the Damascan, the one who has a dramatic, startling revelation; the DaVincian, whose intuitive understanding has always been there; and the Muddler, the one who grows more conscious step-by-step through time. Coming across these personality types helped me understand myself better and the emotional journey that has been triggered by bringing first one damaged little dog, then two, into our world. As I live with the growing knowledge of just how damnably terrible puppy farming is, I recognise the Muddler in me. As someone who takes pride in a certain organised approach to life, it comes as quite the surprise to label myself as such; muddled and me are not easy bedfellows but for the sake of the dogs, I can live with it.

As the shrill call of activism has got louder, I have found myself connecting with others who feel the same, who understand the issues and who care. Some are actively challenging the systems that allow the continuing cruelty, lobbying, sitting through endless rounds of political meetings, chipping away at the networks that fight to keep the status quo. Others are saving dogs, meeting the puppy farmers up close, biting their tongues and keeping cool heads where mine would boil and explode. As I network with others around the world confronting the abusive industry, the grim realisation hits hard that these are big markets where huge numbers of puppies are bought and sold, where parents are abused and bred from, and it never ends for many. My two are truly the rarities that escape to learn what it is to be a dog, not a breeding machine. It is a massive global market of misery. But knowing there are many good people doing good things for dogs in a world that at times seems cruelly, madly awful for them, keeps me *compos mentis*. I am awestruck by the efforts of many and dumbstruck by the slack minds and actions of those who keep the puppy business booming. My efforts at doing something pale beside the hard, gritty, dangerous work done by those on the front line of this battle, for that is what it is.

Braver people than I do this work, often undercover, always in upsetting circumstances. Just reading their emails and accounts at times, I need to take a break and go for a walk with my dogs in the peace of the countryside to clear the images and suffering from my mind. How people do the face-to-face work and retain their emotional wellbeing deeply impresses me. They are truly courageous, especially those who report and speak out about what they see. Some put their names into the public domain and are prepared to take on the many nasty people who would rather they shut up. Many campaigners have been threatened, some have been attacked, but all act with one aim: to be the voice for the dogs that are trapped in a cruel industry.

In my enquiries for this book, people shared shocking experiences of underground rescue operations that they had been involved with to save dogs from abusive situations. A lot I cannot include here but suffice to say anything you read anywhere about the dreadfulness of conditions in puppy farms is true, and represents a tip of the iceberg in terms of the scale of suffering around the world. Many puppy farms never get raided, reported on or closed down. There are just too many around the world. Stories come out of South Africa, Canada, Ireland, Wales, England, Scotland, the United States, Australia, several Eastern European countries, South Korea, Mexico, France – the list of countries complicit in this horrific industry is long. And sadly the campaigners are too few, the puppy buyers too numerous and unaware.

A woman who has dedicated her life to the fight to end puppy farming in Australia and further afield is Debra Tranter. Debra is founder of Oscar's Law, a campaign group aiming to end the factory farming of companion animals and promoting the adoption of animals in rescue. She has been campaigning for over twenty years, exposing puppy farms, rescuing dogs, getting some closed down. She has suffered personal attacks, threats and violence. Yet she fights on. I am in awe of her courage and asked her to describe what it is like going into some of the dreadful places she has been. Debra's brutally honest words are hard to read, they bring home just how tough the work of front-line campaigners and rescuers is:

> Walking into a puppy factory makes you feel like you're on the edge of your sanity. It is so obviously wrong, cruel and unjust and yet legal in almost every country. In Australia we seem to have an 'industry standard' of outside dirt pens surrounded by electric fencing wire to stop the dogs jumping or climbing out, and 'nursery sheds' where the unfortunate mothers are kept lined up for weeks whilst they give birth and attempt to nurture their puppies. Some of these sheds confine between one and two hundred female dogs.
>
> The first thing you notice is the deafening noise of barking which keeps these dogs in a constant state of anxiety; then the stench hits you, and it's a smell that

stays with you long after you have left the sheds.

Walking through the sheds you begin to notice the dogs that are silent, the ones that sit and just stare at the wall terrified that you will make eye contact with them. These are the dogs that have had their spirits broken, so psychologically damaged from years of sensory deprivation they have simply shut down and given up. Some dogs chew at their own skin until it is red raw and bleeding, some spin in circles or pace their small cages in a pattern that's even maddening to watch over and over. They are trapped with no environmental enrichment, stimulation or companionship. It is these dogs that break my heart and keep me awake at night.

When I am at the puppy factory I have learnt to emotionally shut down, just like the dogs do. I see my work as their only chance. I film and photograph their living conditions, trying to find violations to the legislation that will allow me to lodge a complaint. Walking away is harrowing and I feel their eyes on me as I shut the shed door, the precious footage in my hand, hoping it is enough to bring me back to save them.

We have rescued dogs with mammary tumours, skin infections, ear infections so bad that their eardrums have perforated, gum and dental disease from an inadequate diet, prolapsed uteruses, genetic diseases – the list is endless. Unhealthy dogs are still capable of giving birth to puppies. One puppy farmer stated when I questioned her about her dogs' infected eyes, "Dogs don't need eyes to pump out puppies," and in that one sentence she summed up how puppy farmers view what we call companion animals. To them dogs are 'primary producers' capable of making them a small fortune with very little outlay.

In Australia it is legal to confine a dog in a cage for twenty-three hours a day, but there is no one checking if the dogs get their two thirty-minute exercise periods a day. The dogs do not have to be provided with warm soft bedding, only a 'raised bed'. A wooden packing crate or a 44-gallon drum tipped on its side is considered a 'raised bed'. There is no limit on the number of dogs any one puppy farmer can keep, and there are no limits on the number of litters a female dog can have, so she is usually bred from her first season until her body can no longer produce puppies.

It is a brutal, hideous industry, which most people find difficult to understand how it could be legal. I have been investigating puppy factories throughout Australia for twenty years and to me this industry is the ultimate betrayal of our 'best friends'. Our dogs deserve better and they need us to fight this industry – their lives depend on it.

Debra's work is brave and I applaud her for her ceaseless courage and commitment. Changes are afoot in Australia and although slow, there are encouraging signs that a better world for the dogs may be on the horizon. It cannot come soon enough and until it does, Debra and campaigners like her will continue to fight the injustices they witness daily.

14

When Violet Met Susie-Belle

Sing your song. Dance your dance. Tell your tale.
— Frank McCourt, *Angela's Ashes*

We arrived at Primrose Hill early in the morning for the biggest puppy farming awareness day in Europe, Pup Aid. Three years previously, this had been Susie-Belle's first big day out, having only recently come to live with us. Now we were there with Janet, Donna and Beth from the Diana Brimblecombe Animal Rescue Centre (DBARC) to help fundraise, book sign and support the event. The day was forecast warm, but at 7am it was overcast with a threat of drizzle in the air. I had roped in my friend Kathleen to come along for the day as I knew that she would be perfect on the DBARC stall for her ability to talk the hind legs off anyone when it comes to telling them about puppy farming. She is passionate, eloquent and fun to be around, all qualities the day would benefit from. Of almost equal importance for us, she is an excellent cake baker and she had brought along a selection to keep our energy up, our tummies full and spirits sweet during what promised to be a long and tiring day. Beside Kathleen's baked marvels, Michel had taken care of a healthy picnic for everyone and so with our culinary needs met, we were all well set for a great day of meeting people, talking, signing a few books and most importantly having a good day out together.

We had first taken part in Pup Aid when it had been

held near Brighton in the grounds of Stanmer House. Getting Susie-Belle to walk amongst the crowds of people moving from the car park to the event had been a slow and challenging experience as at that early stage, her exposure to people had been limited and everything was new and more often than not, scary. Falteringly she had made her way step by nervous step and we had watched her vigilantly throughout the day hoping we got the balance right as we nudged her along the difficult path to living as a normal dog. Being as new to the experience of helping her as she was to coping with us and her new life, three years further on and a lot more experienced, I don't know if we got it perfectly right that day, but I do know we did not get it all wrong. It was a memorable day for us all but none more so than Susie-Belle; she must surely have wondered what on earth her new life was all about.

Three years on and here she was in London's smart Primrose Hill, subject of a best-selling book, her life bringing publicity to the ongoing problems of puppy farming. Where three years before it had been a task in itself for her to overcome her anxiety about being around people and new places to be able to walk from the car to the event, in London she was eager to be amidst the hustle and bustle. We had brought along a secure pen so that we had somewhere safe to keep the dogs during the day when we needed to, but also to give them a safe, quiet place if they sought it. At home I had thought Twinkle and Susie-Belle would welcome the peace of retreating to the pen, although I accepted Renae would balk at being kept away from the action and insist on being included in every second of the day's activities. I could not have been more mistaken: Susie-Belle objected loudly whenever Michel or I put her on her bed in the pen, mustering her loudest, most plaintive bark to make it obvious she wanted to be out and close to us. This despite being within clear sight and sound of everyone at the front of the stall, as we had placed the pen mere feet away at the back where we thought relative peace might be enjoyed.

Any worries I may have harboured about the day being a bit too much for Twinkle and Susie-Belle disappeared swiftly as I saw and heard how much they both wanted to be in the thick of the action. This was truly different from three years earlier. Our little canine trio were determined to take their places at Pup Aid.

The event was opened by canine celebrity Haatchi and his human best friend Owen, but before they did so, Owen's dad Will brought them over to meet Susie-Belle. Their story – told in the wonderful, internationally successful book *Haatchi and Little B* – is one with sad moments but a happy message, and to meet the pair, and to have Owen cuddle Susie-Belle and her respond in her gentle, loving way was a treasured moment. Owen has a rare genetic disorder, Schwartz-Jampel Syndrome, and Haatchi had a leg amputated after being found as a young dog injured on a railway line – it is suspected he was tied to the track. Their bond is one of pure love and it has touched millions around the world, raising awareness of Owen's rare disorder as well as the beauty of such a close relationship between dog and child. Haatchi is yet one more example of the cruelty of humans to dogs, but more than this, his life story demonstrates the capacity for love that dogs feel, even when they have experienced unimaginable pain from humans. I was delighted to have met them that day, but more than that I was touched to be in the gentle presence of remarkable dogs who have learnt to trust, love and be loved by people despite experiencing the worst that humans can inflict on animals.

Shortly after opening the event, the dog show got underway with a series of fun classes for the dogs to enter. I opted not to take part in anything but the ex-breeders parade with Twinkle and Susie-Belle, preferring to stay with the DBARC stall and help out there. I was also unsure of how Twinkle would react in the ring; her unpredictability could make it more of a trial than a treat for her which was the last thing I wanted. After a mid-morning light rain shower, the sun soon broke through as predicted and by the afternoon the heat was rising, along with the number of people milling around. At one stage it was packed with people and dogs. So many dogs of all shapes, sizes, breeds and mixes. Many people stopped by to have a try at the fun tombola we were running on the stall, some bought books, I signed a few, and many people wanted to meet our little star Susie-Belle, along with her sisters.

With ambassadorial serenity, she grew into her role at Pup Aid, staying calm, content to be in the thick of it, never once showing alarm or tension at the number of people she was meeting. Oh how I wished the puppy farmer who had tied rope around her neck, kept her in the back of a dark and filthy barn and caused her to suffer for years could see her shine at Primrose Hill. An unbroken spirit, a soul well and truly alive; bright, gleaming like *Sirius*. Sirius, the Dog Star, from the ancient Greek '*Seirios*', meaning to glow. Susie-Belle glowed that day all right. She shone, she glimmered, she twinkled. And along the way she lit the path to making the world a better one for dogs in the hearts of many who met her.

Through the day we ate our way through Michel's healthy picnic and Kathleen's calorific cakes and talked to a lot of people. In fact, Kathleen did not stop talking to all who passed. She found her vocation that day, and as adopter of Darcie, one of the most damaged of puppy farm dogs, Kathleen knows plenty about the harm that puppy farming causes. Despite living safely with Kathleen for three years, Darcie still struggles to accept attention, can shoot away in a panic if approached unexpectedly or too quickly and only allows touch from a certain small number of people. Since adopting Darcie, Kathleen has gone on to adopt a second breeding dog, Juno, who joined her canine sisters Darcie and Schnapps shortly after Twinkle came to us. The contrasts and similarities between Darcie and Twinkle are interesting: Darcie, Kathleen's baptism of fire into adopting a dog, is highly touch averse and skittish beyond belief; Twinkle, also touch averse and fearful of unsolicited human approaches, jumpy on a level with Darcie, is reactive but with a high intelligence and ability to learn. Kathleen and I have often wondered if Darcie and Twinkle are related – they look pretty similar and share a lot of characteristics, Twinkle seemingly a milder version of Darcie with her fragile, damaged psyche. Having survived the wild induction into rehoming a rescue dog that Darcie proved to be, Juno has been a much simpler dog by comparison for Kathleen and her partner Mel to live with, although she is not without her problems.

When she arrived at DBARC Juno was severely overweight, weighing in at 16.1 kg (the average weight of a female miniature schnauzer is around 7–8 kg). I met her for the first time on a visit to DBARC and she sat propped up in Janet's office, her belly sprawled in front of her, so fat she was unable to lie down. What misery she must have felt in the harsh environment of the breeding place, no soft cushion to make her difficult repose more bearable. Within a short while, Janet had arranged for her to receive thorough veterinary care and diagnosis and she was found to have Cushing's disease. This affects the body's metabolism and leads to weight gain with a characteristic pot-belly, lethargy, poor exercise tolerance, muscle wastage, hair loss, thirst and frequent urination. It is an unpleasant disease, but once diagnosed, controlled and correctly monitored dogs can live relatively normal lives so long as medication is maintained and regular veterinary care is in place.

Once Juno's Cushing's was under control, Kathleen adopted Juno and agreed to maintain the strict regime she was following for weight loss and activity. Juno could not have found herself in a better home and in the care of Kathleen and Mel she has regained fitness, a healthy weight, has regular check-ups and enjoys life. It is a miracle that she made it out of the puppy farm, as her levels were dangerously high and her weight at a lethal level. To see her now running through woods across the South Downs where she lives, foraging in the undergrowth with a spiritedness only a happy dog could display, it is hard to believe she is the same dog that I saw propped on her Buddha belly. Janet and Kathleen both suspect that she may once have been someone's pet; her familiarity with certain routines and behaviour in the home are atypical of dogs who have lived their entire lives in puppy farms. It is a dreadful, upsetting thought, if true, how Juno must have suffered to have been a pet one day and in a puppy farm the next. This is known to happen, and one reason campaigners advise never advertising dogs as 'free to good homes' is because puppy farmers and backstreet breeders look for these dogs, and if unneutered, use these poor unwanted pets to revamp their breeding stock.

Photographs taken when Juno first joined Kathleen are a graphic reminder of how much damage the puppy farm caused her; with a tummy dropped to knee level, patchy fur and haunted look, her visual transformation within months is astounding. So much so she won a competition run by the RSPCA in the best ex-breeder category, appearing on TV with Kathleen and her immortal line, given to the camera with perfect deadpan delivery: "There is nothing good about puppy farming."

At Pup Aid, photographs of an overweight, unhappy, clearly suffering Juno drew people to our stall and Kathleen talked her head off all day, educating, regaling, hectoring and lecturing the naive, the interested and the simply curious. She captured them with passion and humour and not a person got past her that day that did not hear about puppy farming from the woman who has two dogs damaged by it in markedly different ways. In fact, Kathleen was so effective a communicator that the people on the neighbouring stall from Wood Green, The Animals Charity asked her if she would attend things with them as so many had stopped at their stall after enjoying Kathleen's attentions, having had their minds opened to the idea of adoption and rescue. A fabulous credit to Kathleen and tribute to how her dogs are helping others each time Kathleen speaks of them.

Wood Green is a long-established rescue that has been rehoming animals in London since 1924. Over the years it has opened three more centres, with headquarters now located on its 52-acre site at Godmanchester in the Cambridgeshire countryside. At Pup Aid, with them for the day was Violet from their Godmanchester centre. A beautiful, majestic brown mastiff, Violet was looking for a home having been found on the streets as a stray after recently delivering a litter of puppies. It was obvious looking at her that she had been badly used for breeding and I later found out that their veterinary assessment concluded she had given birth around two weeks prior to being found. This is dreadful – for a mother to be away from her pups is highly distressing and Wood Green described how Violet would anxiously be looking for her babies when she was first in their care. No more details could be found as to the whereabouts of her puppies or where she had been kept and Violet ended up another statistic, just one more abandoned breeding dog, damaged, unloved and homeless. It is only a guess, but she may have been turned out to fend for herself when her value as a breeder was not sufficient to deem her worth keeping. People that breed in this way would care nothing for her life as a sentient being. Her puppies could have been sold to dealers to sell on at greater profit, or direct to puppy buyers, or they may have died. Either way, for Violet, her life as a breeder was over, and being taken in by Wood Green meant that she was at last safe from abuse and people making money from her.

At rescue, she was underweight with skin problems and hip dysplasia, but despite all this and the terrible breeding she had been subjected to, her personality sparkled brightly during her three months being nursed at Wood Green and she touched many with her sweet, mild-mannered nature. As is so often the case, the spirit of abused dogs is stronger than the cruelty man inflicts and in Violet's case, although she was wary, scared and confused as to what had happened to her and her puppies, her inherently loving and playful spirit was not destroyed.

Late during the afternoon, Susie-Belle, a tiny fraction of Violet's size but with a character to match, joined her in an outburst of entertaining play bowing. It was a sight to make the hardest heart squelch just a little: the large brown mastiff with the delicacy of a rapidly deflating hot air balloon, bouncing around in front of the squat, awkward, bunched-up form of Susie-Belle, who was joining in with more woofing racket than graceful movement. Thankfully Violet saved her voice, which I can only imagine is impressively loud, and left the noise to Susie-Belle. This spared the passers-by at Primrose Hill an inevitable startle as they strolled past the big brown mastiff and small noisy schnauzer in the full throes of their awkward, unusual play. Schnauzers make enough noise for all but their most die-hard fans to enjoy and the thought of a mastiff accompaniment is not for the tremulous of heart.

Happily for Violet, she found her new home that day and shortly afterwards went to live with Donna and her family, joining their resident mastiff, two-year-old Red. Violet is the eighth mastiff that has shared Donna's life and for a dog that had a miserable early life, Violet has landed in the most perfect home possible. It is not known how long she has to enjoy life with Donna as sadly, while at Wood Green, ovarian tumours were discovered. However long, the quality of life she now enjoys will more than compensate for a longer life lived in misery, which was once her fate. Her day at Pup Aid, dancing and playing with noisy Susie-Belle, was a special one indeed for Violet, whose life changed forever that day. It is a day so many of us will never forget.

15

Have Dog, Will Travel

The animals of the world exist for their own reasons. They were not made for humans any more than black people were made for white, or women created for men.

– Alice Walker

One of the biggest personal pleasures that has come from writing my first book about Susie-Belle has been the number of many kind people and dogs with similar stories that I have got to know through it. While hearing each story of suffering makes my heart break every time just a little, it is truly moving to know that at least some breeding dogs now have happy lives immersed deeply, at long, long last, in nothing but love. Love that is more than overdue for them but in the cases told to me, it flows in free abundance from full hearts and caring souls. Many of those who make contact now use their own experiences with their special dogs to tell others of the nasty truth festering right at the core of the modern puppy-breeding business. Every time I hear of another person speaking up, sharing their story, my heart repairs and my spirits lift. The abusers have not won. And they will not. The dogs' stories are being told and seeping into the minds of many, so one by one the stories will become a flood and no one will ever again claim not to know that puppy farming exists and is a cruel and nasty business. It will end – soon it will end.

Am I living in a fool's paradise by believing this? Perhaps. But maybe not. The stories are increasing and social media makes it easier than ever before to share them. People are adopting damaged, traumatised breeding dogs and feeling outrage at what their new friends have endured. And they voice that outrage, and the stories increase and circulate wider. The dogs are getting a louder voice; the puppy farmers, abusive breeders, the casually callous making money from breeding their dogs are now talked and written about like never before. The brutality they inflict on dogs is not as easy to hide as it once was. My paradise may be closer to reality than it was before the age of twenty-four-hour news and social media.

One dog in the UK who is using social media to good effect is Lucy, an ex-breeding Cavalier King Charles Spaniel. Adopted in March 2013, Lisa shared with me how she met and adopted Lucy:

> At the time I wasn't looking to adopt a dog but when I saw her picture on a rescue website, and read the story of how she had been used on a puppy farm for many years, I couldn't forget her. I soon realised I wanted Lucy to be part of our family and went about the adoption process. When I went to meet her for the first time, her fosterer had warned me that Lucy was tiny, but nothing could have prepared me for the shell of a Cavalier that I would meet. Lucy didn't even resemble the breed – she was a tiny creature, skin and bones with bald patches to her fur, stained feet from being kept on a urine-covered floor, and an arched back. From a distance she looked like a small puppy. When I first held her it broke my heart as Lucy just wanted to get down and back into her bed.
>
> Lucy has come on leaps and bounds since I adopted her and has turned into a confident, loving little girl who brings joy and a smile to all those that she meets. Unfortunately Lucy does have some health issues: she

has severe dry eye and is almost blind in her left eye. In addition to this, Lucy also suffers with epilepsy, which is a heart-breaking disease as when a seizure strikes all you can do is cuddle them and let them know you are there. I hope it's true when they say dogs live in the moment as I don't want Lucy to ever remember her past. All I can do is give her a home filled with love, which she certainly has.

Lisa shares her life with Lucy on Facebook; their page has many thousands of followers and is a great example of the power social media has to reach out to people who may know little about the suffering of breeding dogs. We met Lucy and Lisa at Pup Aid where there were many remarkable dogs, each with a story to tell if only they could. Another effective user of social and print media we met that day was Angie, with her dog Tilly. Their story is a superb example of how a breeding dog's life can turn around, and Angie, a journalist, with photographer husband Richard, makes sure Tilly's tale is used positively to promote awareness. Here is an insight into their life in Angie's words:

> My desire to have a dog came about as a result of serious health problems and I started to look for a rescue dog at the suggestion of my husband, Richard. I looked at local shelters on the Internet but I'd set my heart on either a Westie or a Parson Russell and even by looking further afield came up with nothing.
>
> Richard suggested searching for 'little dogs' and I soon found a rescue specialising in just that. The first dog on the page was a Westie called Shirley. Along with another Westie, Shirley had been found abandoned on the streets of London. They were in a dreadful condition; filthy, starving and with teeth that were so unclean they were green. They were taken to the pound and were (unknowingly) waiting to be either rescued or destroyed.

At that time, two new foster carers had joined the rescue: Christine and Tony. They went to collect the two dogs on the very day they would have been euthanised. Tony named them Pepsi and Shirley. The two dogs did not get on and so Pepsi went to another fosterer (who later adopted her) and Shirley stayed with Christine and Tony. Settling in with them, she rejected the soft bed they'd bought for the comfort of a crate, which may have felt familiar to what she had previously lived in.

Shirley was taken to the vet's and had a thorough dental examination, including several tooth extractions. The vet said she had certainly been used as a breeding bitch in a puppy farm as she had clearly had many litters, wasn't micro-chipped and guessed that she was about five or six years old as that is when the puppy farmers often throw dogs out – or worse. Christine's blog posts talked of a loving little docile creature who followed her everywhere. There were photos of Shirley sitting with Christine and she appeared to be looking at the laptop screen with her. She looked so cute. I was smitten and applied to adopt her.

We live in Yorkshire. Shirley was hundreds of miles away in Kent but, as luck would have it, we were going to London that weekend and so Christine invited us to meet Shirley.

My first sighting of Shirley was on a railway bridge. She was a shaggy-looking thing and I loved her instantly despite her lack of interest in me. I had never had a dog before and to be honest, I've always been wary of dogs I don't know, but this little creature just exuded love and I didn't know how I'd be able to tear myself away at the end of the afternoon.

When we left, Tony erected a new shed. Christine was very upset when she told me that at the end of the day Shirley had gone into it looking dejected and clearly thinking this was her new home, and she told of the delight Shirley showed when she was encouraged back into the house for dinner.

Thankfully our application endorsed by Christine and Tony was accepted, we passed our home inspection and this little bundle of fluff was soon to be ours. We renamed her Tilly and I went down to King's Cross on the train to collect her two weeks after meeting her.

The first thing that struck me about Tilly was her adaptability. In the hustle and bustle of King's Cross station, she accepted being handed over to me without any fuss at all. She was being as good as gold. She hopped up onto the train and sat on my knee the whole way home. When we arrived, she greeted Richard with much wagging of her tail. It was remarkable. We had got her both a bed and a crate, and because she had been used to sleeping in a crate in the kitchen at her fosterers', we tried to settle her in our dining room. She wouldn't settle and so we brought her up to our room 'just for the night'. She settled in her bed rather than the crate and all was well. By the second night, she was sleeping on our bed and the rest, as they say, is history!

Tilly settled into our lives without any of us missing a stride. Her heartbeat and little tappy footsteps complete our home. Her joyful morning greetings brighten the start of every day. Her companionship, love and loyalty are unwavering and her trust in me is one hundred percent.

Over the past two and a half years, we have watched Tilly become a 'proper dog'. Gone is the timid creature who hid behind my legs, never barked and wouldn't leave my side to go exploring. Now she chases squirrels up trees, barking her little head off. She has even chased seagulls, pheasants and geese – but only from a distance and never fast enough to get close! Her favourite place is the beach but she also loves meadows, woodland and the odd food festival.

Tilly is now a media star – a cover girl for Dog Friendly magazine. We have a column called 'Tilly's Travels', where we travel to luxurious dog-friendly accommodation all over the UK. Tilly also helps me to test travel-related dog products for reviews. We make a great team with Tilly doing the modelling, me doing the writing and Richard taking the photographs. Her story has appeared in several magazines – she really is a superstar.

Wherever we go and whatever we do, Tilly's needs and happiness are our primary concern. When we were lucky enough for her to come and live with us, we vowed that every day we would make it up to her for whatever awfulness she suffered at the hands of other humans – and we do just that.

When I heard how Tilly now enjoys a rich, active life that is shared with thousands, I celebrated yet another victory against those who confine, breed and profit from dogs. She was once made to suffer, then thrown away like rubbish, but survived to be a happy media star with the purest of hearts. Tilly's publicly shared life in beautiful words and pictures provided by Angie and Richard is one where no egos intrude, there are no hidden agendas, just a purity of desire to share a life worth living and writing about. This is campaigning at its best. It engages people and allows them to gently learn the harsh, horrible truth behind Tilly's happiness today. If only her former abusers could know that the dumped dog they threw out on the streets of London now enriches the lives of many. Where they may have damaged her body, they did not destroy her spirit; it shines bright and beautifully amid the luxury of beautiful dog-friendly hotels. Who can fail to find joy in the irony of Tilly's turnaround?

One other thing I love about Tilly's story is that she is a great example of a breeding dog settling into her new life relatively easily. It shows that every dog is totally unique, for

143

she could not be more different from Susie-Belle or Twinkle in how easily she settled. While general guidance is that dogs from puppy farm backgrounds need a steady canine companion to learn from, and this is advice I always pass on, Tilly has done brilliantly with Angie and Richard as an only dog. There are always exceptions to rules, and I am happy to see rules broken when dogs benefit as Tilly clearly has.

There is another, touching facet to their story: Angie was diagnosed with a condition which causes progressive deafness and in April 2011, tragedy stuck when she suffered sudden sensorineural deafness in her 'good' ear, leaving her permanently profoundly deaf. With little hearing remaining in her other ear, she was immediately cut off from everyone around her and while she was still able to speak (and to hear her own voice), she was unable to hear what others were saying. It was a terrifying and isolating time. Bringing Tilly into her life, Angie discovered the unique ability dogs have to heal humans, to offer them just what is needed at the right time. It is often said that we find the dogs we need in life and are as much rescued by them as they are by us. Angie and Tilly epitomise this adage as the bond they have is now so strong, their relationship as close as one can imagine, that Angie proudly says that if she was given the chance to have her hearing restored at the cost of losing Tilly she would not even consider the offer. Knowing that Tilly has suffered badly in the past, yet lives fully in the moment with a state of mindfulness that rubs off on her, Angie says she now spends much of her time smiling, not ruing what she has lost.

16

We Meet A Warrior

*Life's splendor forever lies in wait about each one
of us in all its fullness, but veiled from view, deep
down, invisible, far off.*

– Franz Kafka

When *Saving Susie-Belle* was published, I began receiving
more invitations to talk about puppy farming and our life
together. The motivation for writing anything about our
experiences with our dogs has always been to heighten
awareness of what goes on in commercially driven puppy
breeding today. Along the way, I also like to think it may
encourage others to adopt dogs who are unfortunate enough
to find themselves in rescue. So many great dogs die waiting
for homes to open up to them, for hearts to soften, for people
to be kind and make room in their lives instead of excuses.
Reading about how happy Tilly, Lucy, Violet and others now
are and the joy they bring the humans they live with, who
could not want to enjoy some of that pure pleasure and be
responsible for offering this to other dogs? It is a good reason
to write and talk about adoption.

Writing also provides me with an outlet for the potent
emotions that get stirred when the harsh reality hits hard once
again when I look at what we face in the battle to end puppy
farming. While I cannot do what people like Debra Tranter
do, I can write and I can certainly talk. When opportunities

arise to speak to people and, I hope, influence how they source their canine friends, they are grabbed without hesitation. Any haunting despondency I may feel at what the world is for dogs gets swiftly banished the moment an invitation to speak lands in my inbox. Yes, there are people that want it to be better. Plenty of people. They want to learn about puppy farming, to hear more about Susie-Belle. People do care. Optimism takes over once again and I ping off my acceptance. I find something serendipitous about Susie-Belle's life now inspiring others to join the campaign to end the abuses she endured. To want to meet her, to be in her presence. A dog that for years was seen as nothing more than a wad of cash and when her womb dried up, was thrown out. Little could her former abusers know what the destiny of their discarded 'stock' would turn out to be.

One of my favourite invitations in the first year of publication was to speak at the inaugural Whitstable Literary Festival, WhitLit, in May 2014. Aside from grasping the opportunity to talk about puppy farming, the major attraction for me was that I would get to meet one of my heroes in the dog rescue world, Pen Farthing, founder of the charity Nowzad. I have followed their work ever since stumbling across the story of one man and his mission to save dogs in war-ravaged Afghanistan, shortly after he began his efforts. To share a stage at a literary festival with Pen and the eponymous dog who inspired him to start rescuing dogs in a country that faces so many challenges, was too exciting for me to miss. I felt honoured to be invited and a shade star-struck by Nowzad – far from my typical response to things, being highly allergic to the cult of celebrity.

Pen served in the Royal Marines for twenty years and while on duty in Afghanistan in 2007 he broke up an organised dog fight, not realising the life-changing impact his actions would have on both him and the fighting dog he saved from certain death. Not intending to adopt the dog, nevertheless it was clearly meant to happen and the dog soon got a name, Nowzad, and the world gained a new dog rescuer set on a path to improve the lives of companion animals in one of the most challenging places on the planet to do so. The original aim of Nowzad was to support serving soldiers on the front lines of Afghanistan to rescue the animals they had become attached to during their tour of duty. Hundreds of soldiers have now been reunited in their home countries (USA, UK, Canada, Italy, South Africa, Australia, Holland and Germany) with the dog or cat that adopted them since Nowzad was founded in 2007. But these days, Nowzad works beyond their original aims and their mission statement gives an idea of the incredible vision Pen has for their work:

> To relieve the suffering of animals in Afghanistan, including companion animals, working equines, stray and abandoned dogs and cats and all other animals in need of care and attention, and to provide and maintain rescue, rehabilitation and education facilities for the care and treatment of such animals with no voice but ours.

As well as continuing to adopt dogs for their new families overseas, Nowzad runs what is the first and only purpose-built official dog shelter for strays in Afghanistan, offering a safe, sheltered environment for stray dogs and current soldier animal rescues. There is a small animal clinic and a cattery housing former street cats rescued by locals or soldiers. I have always been impressed with their dedication and commitment to animal welfare, and I was excited to meet both the man and dog behind this remarkable effort. As well as running the charity, Pen is a best-selling author, and thus it was that we were both invited to speak at the Animals in Memoir event at WhitLit.

Susie-Belle and I arrived early in the Kent coastal town to meet up for a pre-talk walk with our friend Zoe and her ex-puppy farm girl Bella and spaniel brother Woody, then just a young pup. Woody, saved from a grim end at the hands of his breeder, shows how disposable some view life that they create. The person responsible for bringing him into the world took him along to the vet with his litter mates to be killed as they were born blind, making them impossible to sell. Fortunately, the vet ensured they were all placed in rescue and since going to live with Zoe, Woody has had cataract surgery and now has normal vision and a full, active life. I can only wonder at how many puppies are bred simply to be killed shortly afterwards when it is realised they are unsaleable due to defects. One might hope that being responsible for the tragedy of a litter of puppies having such brief lives would be enough to deter anyone repeating the risk. Sadly I know this is far from what happens. Some of those who breed have a loose grasp on ethics and will breed on and continue to play Russian roulette with the lives of innocents. This is not speculation; in the course of my research for this book, I have come across enough to know it happens alarmingly often. I have zero doubt it is a regular, if financially regrettable occurrence in the world of commercially driven breeding as the batch of pups are worthless to those who view a puppy's life in monetary terms. A callous disregard for life is endemic in many grubby pockets of the dog-breeding world.

Living nearby, Zoe is a regular visitor to Whitstable, a historic town renowned for its week-long oyster festival held every summer in July. Despite living less than two hours away, this was my first visit, and before heading to the Horsebridge Centre to give my talk, we spent a blowy couple of hours taking in the sea air, wandering the narrow streets, catching up and savouring the literary atmosphere created in the town by WhitLit. It was a great way to clear away any brain fog, and for Susie-Belle to walk off her excitement in time to meet her audience. If she could have known that she was also due to meet the legendary ex-Afghan fighting dog, Nowzad, I am sure she would have agreed that a brisk and windswept walk around town was an ideal way to prepare herself. I was interested to see how the dogs would interact, if at all, and secretly I was much more the Nowzad groupie that day than I let on to anyone. Beyond me being excited about the dogs meeting, I was thrilled to have the chance to be in his presence myself. I have a soft spot for canine heroes that swells to epic proportions when I'm physically with them, much more so than any human hero could ever manage.

As we arrived at the centre, Susie-Belle and I were met by our smiling host, Marnie, and slipped immediately into an easy, relaxed chat over tea with her and Tippi, her beautiful rescue dog. Marnie and her husband had given Tippi, a Staffordshire bull terrier, a home after finding her in rescue; she had been abandoned, tied to a tree in a field and left to an unknown fate. Sipping tea in the Green Room, backstage at my first literary festival, with two dogs, awaiting the arrival of another, all of whom have known cruelty beyond measure, but who now love life, was a great place to be that day. I draw vast inspiration and great warmth from dogs who survive dreadful experiences and not only go on with their lives, but find it within themselves to offer love to members of the same species that had once inflicted pain on them. I felt privileged beyond measure as I sat with Susie-Belle, chatted with Marnie and tickled Tippi, while we awaited Pen and Nowzad's arrival.

We didn't have to wait long as a sudden flurry of activity and excited buzz in the air told us that Nowzad was on his way upstairs to join us. Having read a lot about this dog's life and journey from the grim world of Afghan dog fighting to being the inspiration for a world-renowned dog rescue charity, I was, I admit, completely awestruck as he came into the room. I don't know really what I had expected, although it was somewhere along the lines of a fabled, gentle, cuddly, giant beauty of a dog. My imagination had filtered out the fact that he was a toughened, abused fighting dog when Pen had found him on the streets of Afghanistan. So when he appeared as a lumbering, elderly, wobbly-on-his-legs dog, but Pen still barked instructions not to let Susie-Belle or Tippi approach for their own safety, my fuzzy, woolly, soft imagination got a sudden reality check. For as Pen explained, Nowzad, old as he may have been, was still a dog that had been trained to fight and that had never fully left him. If he decided to resurrect his bad old days, even for a moment, the sheer weight and size of Nowzad would take some controlling. So, despite Susie-Belle being a mere snippet of a dog in comparison, and certainly no challenge, I discreetly slipped her up on my lap, just to be on the safe side. From a respectful distance, we admired the handsome face of this old warrior with his missing ears – cutting them off is common in dog fighting – who was so obviously ageing, laying with his head on his paws, still alert, his eyes calmly, carefully watching all around him. Right there, right then, with Nowzad's powerful energy filling the room, I let my imagination run with what his life had once been, and how remarkable his transformation was. I was slightly giddy with contained excitement with one huge hero on the floor and another little one snuggled on my lap and completely forgot I was about to get up on stage in front of a full house.

After a few minutes, Marnie broke my reverie as she got us all ready to share the Animals in Memoir stage. With Susie-Belle in my arms, Nowzad lying peacefully at Pen's feet and Tippi ably assisting on Marnie's lap, we were led by Marnie through a wonderful hour or so in front of a packed theatre audience, sharing our stories and campaigns. Listening to Pen talk about his work with the Nowzad charity and how the snoozing dog at his feet continued to inspire and drive him, I was awestruck once again at the strength and sheer wonder of dogs. I found it compelling that although Susie-Belle and Nowzad both had dreadful backgrounds for different reasons, their ability to touch the hearts of others, no less Pen and myself, was profound. It was good to talk to the audience about puppy farming, about the abuse of dogs like Susie-Belle purely for money and the things that we can all do to end the market that drives the abuse; but more than this, it was a pleasure to have the chance to demonstrate with the peaceful support and presence of two remarkable dogs that despite all their suffering, they represented the purest majesty of dogs' astounding ability to forgive. Despite coming from different backgrounds and different continents, the similarities between the two dogs were greater than the differences: both had experienced horrific cruelty, in Susie-Belle's case for money, in Nowzad's for sport; both had once been starving and alone, but were now at ease in front of an audience as awe-inspiring ambassadors for a better world for dogs. As I talked and listened, my insides puffed up into a soft meringue of admiration and fondness for them both.

Since WhitLit, Pen and I have stayed in touch. Sadly, Nowzad died a few weeks after we met him and I feel supremely grateful that I met a dog that has left behind such an incredible legacy. Pen spends regular time in Afghanistan and continues to build and expand the work of Nowzad. In 2014 he was the deservedly proud recipient of CNN's Hero of the Year Award for his work reuniting soldiers and their dogs through Nowzad. A perfect tribute to his canine comrade who became an international icon for what can be achieved for dogs, even in the most adverse situations. Although we live completely different lives and I cannot imagine visiting Afghanistan, let alone tackling the huge task Pen has dedicated himself to, we are committed to one common aim that we will do all we can to bring about: a wish that dogs will one day soon never have to suffer for man's selfish, wilful cruelty.

It's really a wonder that I haven't dropped all my ideals, because they seem so absurd and impossible to carry out. Yet I keep them, because in spite of everything, I still believe that people are really good at heart.

Anne Frank, *The Diary of a Young Girl*

17

Let's Talk Puppy Farming

Action is the antidote to despair.

– Joan Baez

Speaking to the audience at WhitLit about puppy farming with Susie-Belle cradled in my arms, her presence a clear example of the real lives that are blighted by a trade fuelled by greed, showed me one thing: public speaking about a wretched but powerful industry is something I can do. I am fortunate that I have never been nervous about public speaking – being a former college lecturer helps – but prior to WhitLit, I had little experience of voicing my opinions on the subject, which might offend some, on the spot. It is one thing to write about it, to share in print not only our lives but my frustrations and emotional angst at the suffering I see caused every day to dogs, but quite another to get up, speak and take questions on it from strangers. As anyone who cares deeply about something will know, emotional subjects can quickly lead to polemical ranting or bad-tempered spats. But in print, what might start life as little more than the demented ravings of an angry, passionate campaigner, usually, before escaping into the world undergoes a crisp edit as I allow calm to settle. I tidy my words, smooth the spikiness, temper my opinions and the polemic is saved for another day. But a public talk is different. No chance to take back what gets said. I am aware my words on puppy farming, especially to those seeking to justify any aspect of it, may boil over into pugnaciousness given the right triggers.

The political activist and writer Susan Sontag once wrote: "Compassion is an unstable emotion. It needs to be translated into action, or it withers." When I came across these words they helped me understand just why I feel such a strong, visceral urge to do something about puppy farming. I am hopeless when things feel unstable, literally as well as metaphorically. I have to change things, I feel driven to act. Having suffered since earliest childhood from a crippling terror of heights, and being prone to attacks of vertigo, the resonance of Sontag's words runs deep for me. Feeling dizzy even when stood on firm ground looking up at a high building is a weirdness I am familiar with and when it happens it is overwhelming. To read Sontag's words and know the compassion I feel for dogs caught up in the breeding nightmare is an 'unstable emotion' if not matched with action, makes perfect sense to me on a literal level. I know I can feel frustrated beyond normal bounds if I am not putting into some kind of motion my overwhelming sense of humanity failing. My writing translates this into what I hope is a useful contribution to bringing in changes and following WhitLit, I knew that not only could I speak out about it publicly, I am compelled to do so; firstly and mainly for the dogs, but also for my own stable mind. Writing and speaking are the actions that I can take. All the time I have a tongue that moves and a working brain to supply it with coherent words, I will speak up. Till it ends for the dogs. Living with dogs that have survived the wretchedness of a business that views and treats them as profit-making machinery is strong motivation to drive me daily to offer any input I can to help bring about its demise.

As I continued to understand what I should and could do to channel what I have into the campaign to improve lives for breeding dogs, I sought out and took up all opportunities to talk about it that I came across. I have always known that Susie-Belle would make a great ambassador for puppy farming survivors as her gentle nature and placid character wins audiences over within moments of meeting her. However, with Twinkle, her unpredictability and somewhat dramatic responses in the first year or so with us made her a less reliable guest. There was no way Twinkle would sit snoozing on my lap, seducing an audience as Susie-Belle was happy to do while I did the talking. It might take me twenty minutes to be able to get Twinkle to sit still long enough to have her harness and lead attached, let alone then snuggle down for a peaceful snooze with a sea of strange faces gazing at her. It's not going to happen.

When Twinkle was involved, any opportunities to speak publicly had to be family affairs; I needed Michel along as an extra pair of hands and eyes. Twinkle also takes reassurance from having both sisters with her and in any new situation does better if they are nearby. So it was with pleasure, but a touch of trepidation, that I accepted an invitation for all of us to attend a Miniature Schnauzer Club Fun Day in Northampton early on in Twinkle's second year of freedom. At this stage she was markedly calmer a lot of the time, and was making steady progress on a day-to-day basis. Little challenges to her routines were successfully worked through and in the main accepted and I was confident enough that with Michel giving me a hand with the three dogs, even if it was a busy environment, all would be well. It promised to be not only a chance for me to talk about puppy farming, but also a good day for us all to share in and we hit the road early to arrive in good time.

On arrival, a noisy miniature schnauzer rout welcomed us. This was after all a fun day for a breed with a reputation for boisterous loud greetings and as we stepped from the car, I knew we had arrived at the right place. After a rowdy meet and greet amongst the many dogs and humans that had arrived, the event got underway. There was a mix of activities going on, both in the hall and outside, where fun agility and games were taking place. Inside, the hall was large and noisy with people and dogs mixing and mingling, some chaotically, others calmly; all riotously normal for schnauzer meets. Only for us, more used to outdoor canine gatherings, the enclosed space, with its bustling, hectic atmosphere, was a touch overwhelming, particularly for Twinkle. Forced into close proximity with shuffling feet and scraping chairs on a noisy floor, and too many people all around her, she was not a happy dog. As people began settling themselves down in front of the stage, Michel found a quieter spot towards the back to sit with Renae and Twinkle, hoping to give her a little peace away from the hurly-burly. Scooping up Susie-Belle, who was also beginning to be bothered by the frenetic atmosphere and rising cacophony, I moved to the front to give my short talk. It wasn't quite as I had planned as I battled to be heard at times over what may have been considered by some to be the more interesting noises coming from the canine members of the audience. Nevertheless, with Susie-Belle in my arms, I attempted to give my spiel about puppy farming, why I had written the book and what Susie-Belle had survived. In a hall full of beautifully happy dogs, almost all of whom had known nothing but love and care in their lives, it was a sobering reality for many in the audience to hear the truth of what lies behind a lot of puppies being sold today.

After what passed for my talk and signing a few copies of the book, Michel and I headed outdoors to chat to people and enjoy what was turning out to be a beautiful summer's day. I did more talking outside in the sun, one-to-one with interested individuals, than in front of the audience. All was good: the message was out our trip was worthwhile. While Renae seemed unperturbed by the boisterous excitement all around and Susie-Belle was happy in my arms, having Michel with me to help our sensitive girl, Twinkle, was essential. Moving into the open air and away from the bustling atmosphere in the hall definitely helped settle her. Sitting under the trees together, watching from a distance the enjoyment being had by everyone with their dogs, Michel and I reflected on how hard it still was for her to cope in situations that were new, especially where there was any degree of disorder or clamour. She has always been quite different from Susie-Belle in this regard and nothing can ever be taken for granted with Twinkle. While she may appear to be calm and getting on with whatever it is we are doing, suddenly her real emotions can surface and we know that she is not coping. Sometimes we know the trigger, other times it can occur unexpectedly. As I spend a lot of time with her, I can spot early warning signs and take action to avoid causing her upset. At the fun day, I knew it might be more of a challenge than she was capable of meeting, but days out in novel places are also important for her, especially with her sisters alongside to smooth the way. With Michel there to help, I thought we could do it right, and it would contribute in a small way to her developing into the dog I know she can be. Small challenges certainly do allow her to use her brilliant brain, to engage her faculties, rather than leaving her trapped by her fears. Tempting as it may be to protect her from all novelty, all challenge, by doing so, we risk preventing her from growing, developing into an ordinary dog with extraordinary qualities; one capable of living, enjoying an ordinary life. It is getting the balance right that is our great responsibility.

Aside from all of this going on in my head when I received the invitation for the day, and it being a chance for me to talk about puppy farming, there was another reason I had been happy to accept the invitation: I would get to meet another survivor of puppy farming, Marnie, who would be going along to enjoy the event. Marnie's adoptive family had been in contact with me since reading the book and were keen to meet up.

Peggy and Graeme had given Marnie a home after she had been rescued from a notorious puppy farm in their area. When we met, she had been living with them for a few months and was making good progress. When she first arrived in their lives she was, like many from her background, highly traumatised and terrified of all humans. Having only recently been rescued, she was underweight, with a thin, poor coat. Distressingly for Graeme and Peggy, in the early days, much of the time she cowered in fear and without fail if approached; she crawled, rather than walked and would let no one near her, running off whenever anyone attempted to stroke her. Like many dogs that have lived as she did, Marnie would sit staring fixedly into space for no apparent reason, unresponsive to those around. The day they took her home, Peggy gave her a soft toy for comfort, but when Marnie picked it up, it emitted a high-pitched squeak, whereby she dropped it and shot into the corner of the room, tail down, where she stayed, whimpering. Peggy ensures no toys she now has have squeakers as Marnie still finds the noise upsetting, a noise suggested by her vet may trigger memories of distressed puppies.

None of this was apparent at the fun day, and although still nervous around people, when with her family, Marnie had clearly learnt to accept their love and gentle care. While Twinkle was twitching around in the hullabaloo of the hall, struggling to cope with it all, Marnie lay on her back on Peggy's lap enjoying a calming, meditative massage on the back row of seats. It was really a delightful scene, a dog so unused to touch and human contact relaxing in the safe hands of those now offering nothing but love. I watched in complete admiration of the total trust that exists between Marnie and Peggy.

We spent a pleasant few hours outside, getting to know more about Marnie's life. As we knew it would be, all dogs got along beautifully, happy in one another's company as we sat in the shade of the trees enjoying lunch. But stroking Marnie's velvety soft ears, I was shocked as my fingers slipped through a gaping hole in the ear flap. It was an old injury that must have occurred at some stage in the farm and I dreaded to imagine the pain she must have endured as it was no doubt left untreated. As well as this, Marnie had several missing teeth, which according to her vet, looked like they had been lost following severe trauma, likely a kick in the face. Like so many other breeding dogs, Marnie had certainly suffered during her years of confinement, producing puppies, making money for her captors. But she is safe now – loved, safe and free, and meeting her, seeing how well she now is, was a highlight of our day.

At the end of the event, as I went inside to present a prize, leaving Twinkle with Michel, the pressure of the day revealed itself as she managed to flip herself out of her harness in a lightning moment of panic which struck without warning – something she had not done for a long while. Her heightened stress response that day reminded us once again that contrary to what she shows to the outside world most of the time, Twinkle's inner demons are still present, lurking within, perversely clinging onto her psyche. At the first opportunity, when her protective calm is chipped, her fears burst through. Through our daily routines, keeping things steady for her, she can protect herself from the injury that her past still threatens. It may never be over for her, it just gets a little less injurious, her essence becoming a little more protected as we travel the long journey to some kind of happiness with her.

We headed home at the end of the day with one puppy-farming survivor doing brilliantly well three years after leaving the puppy farm, and the other, into the second year of her life of normalcy, it would be more accurate to say was just coping well. Coping with being free.

18

Where Now?

We turn not older with years but newer every day.
— Emily Dickinson

As I write this, Susie-Belle has been out of the puppy farm exactly four years and Twinkle two. During the time they have both been with us, they have brought us much happiness, a few challenges and set me on a path of campaigning that I will not leave till puppy farming ends. It may mean that I spend my whole life campaigning, or it may be much quicker than that. Who can know? The optimist in me thinks that changes, real changes, are around the corner. There are signs that things may be improving slowly, far too slowly for my liking, but nevertheless the signs are there that politicians are being forced to address the issues of dog breeding and welfare. Not just in the UK but around the world. As more and more people become aware of what puppy farming means for parent dogs as well as the puppies, it is getting harder for legislators to ignore the public calls for things to improve.

Over the course of the past couple of years researching this book, I have made many good friends and acquaintances around the world, all people involved in their own battles, all sharing the same goals. I have come to understand that it is only when the true global picture of commercial-scale puppy breeding is recognised that matters will improve for the dogs who are caught up in it. For if we look only at our own country's problems, whether we be in the United States, Canada, Australia, South Africa, the UK, or elsewhere, the industry will move off and still be a problem for the dogs, just not a problem on our own local doorstep. That is not good enough for me. Here we have huge problems with puppy farms located across the British Isles, yet dealing with those alone just leaves open the importation of puppies from European farms, which is already being recognised as a terrible catastrophe for dogs.

One thing that I have noticed over the past year is a groundswell of public engagement with the problem. Social media is a terrific aid to all of us actively campaigning, investigating and trying to effect change. Real change – not just superficial, tickle at the surface and hope it goes away change that politicians up until now have relied upon. No, what is happening now, facilitated by people's use of social media, is that the atrocities that are being done to dogs in the name of puppy breeding are no longer able to be hidden from sight. And more people are getting angry, sad, frustrated, engaged, and demanding their politicians properly act to improve things. This groundswell is growing, and the solidarity amongst those of us who care around the world – and we are many and increasing in number – is starting to produce many small but strong shoots of hope that this awfulness in the name of convenience and commerce may soon end for the dogs.

As well as social media, there are increasing blogs being written, articles being published and news and TV documentaries being aired. Set for worldwide release, a US documentary film that exposes the connections between the agricultural industry, regulators and puppy breeders in the United States may well be the film that really catalyses global change. *Dog By Dog* has the potential to change the game for breeding dogs not only in the United States but around the world, as the connections will be seen by viewers to be the same in many countries; it is merely the specific national agencies that differ. Having closely watched the development of the documentary for some while after initially being contacted by one of its producers, Karen Doonan, and being privileged to connect with the film-making team, I see it as having the power to end puppy farming around the world. At the very least it will make the business a lot less easy for those involved. It will no longer be possible for those in the web of power to remain anonymous, as they have been to all but experienced campaigners who have known about the connections for a long time.

The viewers, the puppy-buying public, those who provide the market, who want their convenience-bought puppies, will see that the puppy industry is nothing about a love for the dogs, but all about a love for the money that can be made from them. Money that goes to big corporations as well as small businesses and individuals. Money that is made from the suffering of millions of parent dogs around the world. The cruelty and greed inherent in the industry have been largely hidden from public awareness. Till now.

With all this happening, it is a time where pressure needs to be maintained on politicians – they need to know that these issues matter to their voters. Voters who will no longer be content to be politely fobbed off. We need to hold them to account for promises made, if and when they make them. And when they refuse to even promise to do better by the dogs, we have to keep pressing them to act for us. To do the right thing for our companion animals. Engagement in the political process is an essential requisite for all those who will no longer turn a blind eye or accept the status quo. All of us can use our political systems to get legislators to act. It is only through effective legislation, plus enforcement of the laws, that puppy farming will be forced to change.

Of course, this must go hand in hand with us all, each and every one of us, telling puppy buyers what we know. For the buyers are also responsible – the puppy farmers, backstreet breeders and plain greedy breeders who are driven by the easy money they can make are supplying a market that is there and booming. In the words of one puppy farmer, "Demand outstrips supply." There has to be a multi-pronged approach to ending this misery for dogs like Susie-Belle and Twinkle and all the others who never get a name, never know a life beyond the cage, barn, shed, or back room. Engagement in all aspects has to happen and it is happening. We can all take our place in the campaign and do what we can to help the dogs. They cannot liberate themselves from this industry – we need to do it for them.

While I sense there is great change on the horizon around the world, I know a lot of dogs still suffer and will end their days never knowing love. Dogs just like Susie-Belle, who was fortunate, finally after much abuse and awfulness, to find her way out to a new life, one which she nowadays wholeheartedly enjoys. She may be getting older and stiffer and some days not have as much verve as we'd like her to, but there is no doubting that she has a deep desire to enjoy each day that she now lives in freedom. She may have spent the majority of her life in captivity, but life for her is *now, now, now*. Her vivacity brightens every day we share with her. We do not dwell on her age or the years spent before coming to us, years of loneliness and pain, we choose to look at her each day as she now is, share in her happiness and count ourselves lucky to be blessed with her in our lives.

> For age is opportunity no less
> Than youth itself, though in another dress,
> And as the evening twilight fades away
> The sky is filled with stars, invisible by day.
> – Henry Wadsworth Longfellow, *Morituri Salutamus*

Twinkle continues to work hard to get to where her sister now is and every week that passes she makes small steps which show us she is accepting the odd feelings of happiness she now recognises. The moments of calm become longer and more obvious and we grow steadily more companionable as a unit. Although I have always deeply desired this for Twinkle, it is only recently that we sense that she knows that this is even possible. That this is what she can be: a beloved companion who is here for herself; not us, but her. When I imagine how it must have felt, and probably still does for her some days, not to know what being companionable feels like, it saddens me. But, then I see her settle down, a soft sigh escaping, one that sounds suspiciously like contentment, and any haunting sadness is quickly dispelled.

Some days are great and with a hippety-hop she leaps a few steps farther down the road to being properly happy. Others, we take a slide backwards, but all are good for her now: she is journeying, travelling forwards to find her real self. It has been several weeks now since she was minded to run up the stairs to get away from me when the harness needs putting on to go out. Most mornings she sits neatly on her bed, allows me to crouch down to her side and gently brings her face closer to mine as I slip the harness on; then with a soft brush of her face against mine, I know we are good. She expresses herself more each day and barks and barks at me sometimes to get me to do something, to understand her – which I still don't a lot of the time. But together we have our way of muddling along, puttering through our days, enjoying a life spent quietly shared between England and France, and I know she is doing her best to embrace what life now offers her.

So as we continue our lives together, taking each day as it comes, filling each one with as much peace, freedom and contentment as we can for the dogs, we do so in the hope that one day, there will be no more to save. That all dogs will be as loved and free as ours are.

The only way to deal with an unfree world is to become so absolutely free that your very existence is an act of rebellion.

– Albert Camus

Epilogue

As my involvement in issues around puppy farming and animal rescue has deepened I have come to understand for myself just how thoroughly, damnably hard the lives of many dogs are in our society. A society that claims to love animals. Britain is glibly said to be a 'nation of animal lovers'. That is an old myth, a claim that was never more untrue than now, when we look at the thousands and thousands of dogs and cats alone that are euthanised each year simply because there are too few people willing to offer them a home. Dogs who languish in shelters having been bought as puppies, messed up by owners who do not give them what they need to be dogs; do not give them the time, attention, training and help needed to live as happy dogs, and then dump them for someone else to deal with. All the while this is going on, the pet industry is thriving around the world. It is a billion-dollar business where ridiculous sums of money are spent by people on consumer goods for their pets, on items the animals don't need or care for. The pet clothing industry alone is massive. Dogs are dressed up and made to look more like children or toys than dogs. There is something insane to me about all this when we step back and look at the huge numbers of healthy dogs killed because they are homeless, and the dogs like Susie-Belle and Twinkle being forced to supply the trade in puppies.

One thing that would help to rebalance things in favour of the dogs would be for more people to consider rehoming a dog. Or two, or three. Not buying a puppy. I hope the booming puppy business will reach its peak someday soon, and a sense of morality returns to understanding what having dogs in our lives is really all about. They are individuals that offer us so much and demand so little. It is not about dressing them up, treating them like children, or worse, toys, the novelty of which always wears off at some point, it is about respecting dogs for being just what they are: remarkable, wonderful animals who have evolved alongside man to be perfect companions. Lifetime companions. Not until the next fad or fashion comes along. The old, the homeless, the damaged, the ugly, the less than perfect, they are all utterly wonderful dogs who deserve good homes more than puppy farmers deserve the money they can make from breeding more puppies that will be discarded down the line. Any campaign against puppy farming has to include strong advocacy for rehoming dogs and it is something I feel increasingly passionate about as I see that drastically reducing the demand for puppies is essential.

Here are a few thoughts on what is an essential side to the anti-puppy-farming message, thoughts that I share in the hope that readers might take them on board and help to improve the image and prospects of rescue dogs, the role of rehoming centres and by doing so, hit the puppy farmers hard. By one dog being rehomed it takes one puppy sale away and it affects the industry. If we all did this, or at least promoted it and helped others to do it, the industry would be brought to its knees. Consumers are keeping the puppy business booming. Changing consumerist attitudes to dogs will help end it.

When we decide to bring a dog into our lives, a lot of people go puppy buying. Heading out to our local animal rescue centre to look for our new friends is not considered often enough, despite the fact that there is every chance that the perfect dog will be found there, patiently waiting for someone to come along and take them home. This is a massive shame, both for the dogs that have to stay patient for longer, or lose their lives waiting, but also for the families that miss out on these dogs, who have deep wells of love they have been storing up while waiting for a new family to share it all with. Dogs love to love even if they are temporarily homeless. I think that a lot of people misunderstand what adopting a dog involves. They too readily focus on the challenges and overlook the rewards. People quickly say rehoming isn't for them as they don't want the trouble of someone else's problem dog, or they don't want to be asked questions by the rescue, or judged, they just want to hand over their cash and bring home a puppy. This is sad, as so much misunderstanding, so many myths, wrong ideas and impatience drive the puppy industry and damage the chances of millions of homeless dogs.

Although adopting a dog may not be possible for absolutely everyone who wants to share their life with a dog, it really is possible for us all at least to consider doing so. Often people think that rescue centres only have older dogs and no puppies but this is far from the truth. Sadly, many female dogs end up in rescue centres when their owners discover they are pregnant and deliver their puppies whilst there. Those puppies are then available for adoption and make perfect pets, once the ideal families come along to give them that chance. Puppies also end up in rescue when owners have bought them impulsively, without thinking about the work that a puppy involves, quickly giving up and handing them over to others. This happens all the time and is an example of why impulse avenues for puppy buying, like pet shops, should be outlawed. Puppies are too often bought on a whim without thought and it is an unpleasant truth that puppies lose their cute appeal pretty quickly for many in society.

Start talking about rescue and shelter dogs and many people automatically, without any real thought, dismiss the possibility of taking one into their lives, believing that being in rescue must mean the dog is troubled or will be trouble. Again, far from true. Dogs land in the laps of rescuers for many reasons, most often none of which are to do with the dogs themselves. Our modern society is tough for dogs and reasons for dogs ending up in rescue reflect this: marriage breakdown, housing issues, change in working lives, death or illness of owners, inability or unwillingness to train, bad choice of breed for lifestyle or experience, or just plain boredom with the puppy that is no longer cute, all commonly lead to dogs being put up for rehoming. While some dogs do have behavioural issues, they are so often created by circumstances, a lack of socialising, training, effort and commitment on the part of their previous owners. Good rehoming centres properly assess dogs in their care and offer adoptive families help, support and backup to work through any issues.

Far from all this being a dragging nuisance for the new owners, it can be a great experience and uplifting stories abound from those who find themselves growing in unexpected ways through the journey with their newly rehomed friend. Dogs require commitment, effort and understanding, whether they start their life with us from puppyhood, or when older. Great dogs languish in rehoming centres, their only problem being that they are homeless – not damaged or troublesome at all.

People often fear an inquisition when they think about adopting a dog and are not willing to have a rehoming centre scrutinise their life and cast judgement on their suitability. I find this a curious reason people give for not considering adoption over buying. The reason good rescues go through detailed assessments is that it helps to match the best pet for the circumstances. Why people assume that rescues will be happy to just hand over a dog without scrutiny, I don't understand. I hear people get cross that with so many dogs needing homes, are the rescues not just happy that someone comes along and offers a home? Well, no. Rescues put the animals' needs first and need to be certain the home being offered is the right one. By going through a detailed assessment, it helps to ensure that for both dogs and humans involved, adoption is a success.

If the assessment from rescues is off-putting, decent breeders will do much the same with any potential puppy buyers – if they don't and are willing to sell a puppy without scrutinising the life they are going to share, then alarm bells should be ringing loud and clear, as no good breeder cares so little about where their puppies are off to that they don't bother to inquire, scrutinise and judge. Much like good rescues. They will also make puppy buyers wait. If you can see a puppy for sale, go and buy and take it home that day, you are not buying from a great breeder. You are buying from someone who wants the sale.

The much feared and all-important home visit check that many reputable rescues insist upon can be a great asset in helping potential adopters see their home from the dog's perspective. This is especially the case for novice owners who may not have much clue as to what makes a good, secure environment. Dogs can slip out of the tiniest opening, or leap seemingly high fences. Suggestions can be made to adopters which can avoid the unexpected and heart-wrenching accidents and escapes from happening. Again, if a puppy breeder shows little or no interest in the home environment, those screaming alarm bells should be going off. *There should be little difference in the scrutiny between a breeder and a rescue if taking one of their dogs.* It should be embraced, not knocked.

Another reason people will dismiss rehoming as an option is that they fall in love with a particular breed. This is something that Michel and I fully relate to. We adore our little gang of miniature schnauzers and my agonising grief when we lost Jasmine, our first, drove me straight to finding another miniature schnauzer puppy, Renae. People mistakenly think that pure-bred dogs will not be found in rescue. This is again far from the truth in a society where dogs are bred and discarded with an ease that has never been seen before. Purebred dogs and those with sound pedigrees find themselves handed into rescues. So, for those who do their homework on which breed is right for their lifestyle and set their heart on their particular breed, buying a puppy is not the only way to bring one into their lives. As well as centres and shelters, there are breed rescue groups up and down the country seeking homes for dogs. A bit of time and effort and homework is all that is needed.

Dogs cost money throughout their lifetime, which we all hope will be long and happy, and trying to get a bargain at the outset is not the ideal mindset. Buying a puppy cheap is likely to be setting owners up for costly veterinary bills down the line. Well-bred puppies are expensive for good reason. But even cheap puppies cost more than most rehoming adoption fees. So although saving money is not the sole reason to consider adoption, it is a pragmatic one. As well as the lower adoption fee, rehomed dogs will usually already be microchipped, vaccinated and neutered (if not, ask why not and be wary), all saving significant money.

The simplest way to avoid giving business to the puppy farming industry is by rehoming a dog. That way, we can at least be certain that we are not supporting a business that churns out puppies for easy cash with no scruples as to the welfare of the puppies or their parents. It is the only way that the puppy trade will slow up and be less lucrative for those who currently make easy money literally off the backs of suffering dogs.

If you take one message from this book, and I hope you take many, the one message that needs to be shared far and wide is that it is puppy buyers who are keeping the puppy farming business going. It is the puppy buyers waking up to the part they are playing in causing misery for dogs like Twinkle and Susie-Belle, that needs to happen. The responsibility has to be placed where it lies. Only then will the dogs be free to live as dogs.

Adopting a Survivor

What to Expect and How to Help

It is tempting to imagine that when rescued from breeding places, dogs finding themselves in their new, loving homes will feel instant gratitude and demonstrate this to their new human companions. This is not the case. They do not know how to accept love and must be taught, and ideally learn from the steady, affectionate canine members of the household. They need to be given the time and patience to grow into themselves as dogs that are free to be just this: dogs. Until this point in their lives they have been treated as a machine and lived lives of utter misery.

While each one that comes out of a commercial breeding environment is an individual with unique characteristics and needs, there are some common behaviours that might be displayed. It is useful for anyone offering a home to one of these special but traumatised dogs to be aware of these. Furthermore, there are some key actions that can be taken that will help the transition from abused breeding dog to the much loved companion dog they deserve to be. For some the transition will be relatively quick, a matter of months, for others, it will take years and some may never fully overcome their past. But they will see each day what it means to be loved and each day their hearts will heal a little more, they may just never be able to show it.

I offer the following information and guidance, with

permission from and great thanks to Janet North and Donna Penfold of the Diana Brimblecombe Animal Rescue Centre, the volunteers and campaigners that make up Stop Puppy Farming End the Cruelty (SPEC) and Terri Walters from Safehaven Small Breed Rescue – all highly experienced individuals who have graciously provided much of this sound advice in the wish to help more dogs.

Arriving in Their New Home

It is important that dogs taken from puppy farms, where they will have been confined in small spaces, are given their own 'safe' place in your home. Ideally this is a crate with cosy, soft bedding and blankets. Place the crate in a quiet area, away from traffic flow in the house, but not away from the usual space where you spend time with your dogs. It helps them to observe from their safe spot your usual routines and interactions with your pets. Giving the new dog the opportunity to go in and out of the crate as they choose is essential. In the early days, they will retreat a lot to their safe place and begin to feel a sense of themselves within your household and family. As time goes by, their need to retreat will lessen, but keeping the crate and bedding available for longer is important. They are emotionally fragile and expected to cope with enormous continual challenges in their first few weeks and months. We can help minimise this by maintaining some constancy in their new lives by leaving their safe place as just that. Do not rush to remove it or force them to share other beds if they do not choose to.

Some people find that covering the crate at night helps the dogs settle. This is sometimes a difficult thing to accept as we have a natural desire to give them full freedom. If you find your dog is restless in the first few nights, it may be that the freedom is too overwhelming and covering the crate may help them feel secure.

House-training

Dogs from breeding environments are not house-trained.

Most males will mark in the home, as do some females. Begin house-training straight away by establishing a routine, going outside every couple of hours or so and allowing plenty of time for them to eliminate. They are generally terrified when outside and need time to overcome this.

Some act quite differently during the hours of darkness as they may have never seen daylight. Very many have also never seen grass, and will be scared to even step on it. Be prepared to go into the garden with them in all weathers, on a lead if necessary. However, as it is unlikely they have ever been on a lead, they may panic when they feel any collar pressure. A body harness and trailing line will help in these circumstances.

While some will learn quickly, for others it may take months; if there are resident dogs in the household, this helps greatly as they can follow their example. Be patient – never scold or raise your voice when accidents happen. Remember they will have soiled their living spaces for years as they had no option. This is their norm, even though it is far from normal behaviour for dogs.

Eye Contact

Although it is understandable that we wish to cuddle them and propel them with full-hearted demonstrations of affection towards a better place, this is not what they need at this stage when they first begin their new lives. It may be a very long time before cuddles are anything other than terrifying. It may never change. Do not foist yourself on the dog. When they first arrive, ignore their presence and avoid making eye contact. Many abused dogs refuse to make any eye contact with humans. This indicates fearful submission, which decreases as the dog comes to realise we will not harm them. Forcing eye contact will not help.

The easiest way to ignore their presence is to understand why we have to. In the puppy farms, when humans are around the only sounds these dogs hear from humans is shouting or banging metal poles on cages; they will also be aware of the noise of distressed barking that comes from other sheds or barns. But there may be no barking from the shed or barn where the humans are, because the dogs in this particular barn, at this particular moment, are living in terror of being paid attention. Attention brings pain, attention snatches their puppies away from them. Attention brings nothing but misery.

Early on, the dog may carefully follow you around the house, but as soon as you turn around, even with no eye contact, the dog will run away back to their bed, and then when your back is turned, they will be there, following you. In time the dog will learn to trust you and begin to look into your eyes, but it will only happen when they are ready.

If you already have a dog, stroke and quietly give affection to him or her without looking at your new addition. The look of amazement on the face of an ex-breeder watching your dog approach and enjoy being touched or engaging in play with you is priceless.

Fear of Human Hands and Approach

Throughout their lives, breeding dogs are never petted or shown any affection. The only time most dogs are removed from their cages or pens it is a painful experience. The dog may be grabbed by the first part of their body that is reached: tail, legs, scruff, ears. Their fear of being grabbed is sometimes overwhelming and they may flee if they suspect this is about to happen.

After giving the dog plenty of time in their new space with you, where they are allowed to just settle and see your normal interactions with your pets, it is appropriate to begin to help them to gain trust in you. How quickly you do this depends entirely on the dog. It could be several days. Take your cue from him or her, observing the body language and noting any signals of stress, or attempts at calming themselves, like lip-licking, avoidance of eye contact or yawning (when not tired). Do not rush the dog. When ready to begin slowly, gently gaining their trust, move quietly and smoothly and lie down on the floor with your eyes averted to allow the dog to settle and approach in their own time. Do not invade their space and never put yourself in their "safe place". Let the dog come near you and sniff. It may take an hour or days for this to happen.

To get the dog used to human touch, it can sometimes be good to begin with gently but confidently holding the dog, stroking them softly for a few seconds, speaking quietly and then placing them carefully down before panic sets in. This is not going to be appropriate for all dogs early on. Touch-averse dogs will hate handling and if you rush this stage too early in their development, it will set them back. Once again, take your cue from your dog; be sensitive to what you are being told. It is important they know they are not being restrained and can get away when they choose. If handling is tolerated, lengthen the time for this ritual each day but do not force it. Be highly sensitive to the limits of tolerance the dog has. Keep everything in the environment calm and quiet during this adjustment period. Make it a peaceful, special time that may only be for a few seconds, but which will start to allow the dog to know human touch is good. It takes time for them to realise they are not going to be manhandled or mistreated.

Often they will cower when you approach and, through fear of being kicked or hurt, will avoid passing you at all costs. If you do approach, and they are backed into a corner, with (in their mind) no escape route, then it is likely their bladder will release. It can be deeply upsetting when this happens; to realise our approach can cause such fear and sheer terror in the dog for whom we offer nothing but loving compassion. But do not fuss. It happens. And one day, it won't.

If possible, as well as their safe place, let them lie on a couch or somewhere off the floor. Raised beds are great as they can feel more vulnerable when close to the ground, especially when approached. If this is the case, when approaching, get down to their level. Always remember that their responses are not aggressive – their spirit has been broken.

Feeding Behaviours

In the puppy farm, any time the cage or pen door is opened, fear is the response because a cruel human is behind it. Of course, the cage door must be opened to insert a bowl of food which may also be used to entice the dog within reach. It is not unusual for survivors to run in the opposite direction when we place their food down.

While they may quickly learn to eat from a bowl, often they will be too frightened to leave their bed to eat or drink, no matter how hungry or thirsty. For some, a little hand-feeding from their bowl will help, while for others this will terrify them. Be sensitive, experiment and find which options help. Do not press forward if what you do is not welcomed.

Some will need you to stay in the room while they eat. Avoid watching them, turn your back and wait until the dog feels safe enough to eat. Leave them to eat undisturbed. They will usually eat quickly, eyes darting everywhere, constantly watching the environment, back legs stretched out as far as they can possibly go. Should you move slightly or a noise is heard they may well abandon their food. If you have other dogs, it can help to feed your new dog in its own place away from the rest of the dogs, as some will not eat if another dog comes near. Again, observe what happens and adjust as needed without fussing.

Fear of Noises

All noises can be frightening. Sometimes what to us is the most benign may be terrifying, yet what we may assume will scare, doesn't. Household noises may be highly alarming to some dogs and not others – a vacuum cleaner, a washing machine, an electric kettle, even the rattling of keys – although for some reason, many survivors like watching television, cartoons in particular, oddly.

Try to keep voices in the home gentle – this is especially important when doing anything with the dog, for example feeding. Chatting to the dog is good, but remember they have lived with the sounds of aggressive voices (often male), so keep the chatter light and soft. And remember, no eye contact – eye contact means attention, and attention is scary. As long as eye contact is avoided while chatting, the dog will relax slightly, because they will feel no attention is focused on them and will gradually get used to the normal sounds of life within a home and realise that a gentle voice is no threat.

Flight Risk

All dogs from this background are high flight risks. Never take your dog outside a secure area without a well-fitting, secure harness. There is every chance that should the dog escape or wriggle out of a harness they will run until they collapse; catching them may be impossible. Prevention is the best solution. As your relationship together strengthens and bonding deepens, the risk lowers, but this can take many months.

Most have never been taken for a walk and are more at ease with a harness than a collar. The majority have never actually had the chance to run, only ever being kept in a shed, pen, or small run. Getting them used to wearing a harness and lead is best done inside the house. Allow the lead to trail so that they get used to the sensation before taking them outside.

Walking them on extending leads is not recommended as accidentally dropping this and it clattering near the dog can cause the dog to bolt and disappear and be impossible to capture. Remember they are easily spooked and a high flight risk for quite some time. Take your time learning the limits of what your dog can cope with outside the house, keeping them secure at all times.

Getting them used to being outside is scary for us and them in the early days, but find quiet, safe and secure places and gradually show them the world outside the home is there to be explored. Take it slow and steady and gradually their natural curiosity will replace their fears. Build daily, regular routines of going outside together. Being on walks with us helps to establish bonds, engage their senses and encourages them to develop their personality over time.

Fear of Hoses

Water hoses frighten many breeding dogs. The reason is because often pens and cages are hosed down with the dogs still present. Hoses are also used to punish dogs for barking.

Fear Biting

Fear biting is more common in abuse cases than in puppy farm survivors, but it can certainly happen. The vast majority of all dogs who bite do so out of fear. Breeding dogs, like feral ones, usually cower in the presence of humans. Fear biting can frequently be overcome with proper commitment and time to build their confidence and allow them to work through the multiple issues they are burdened with through their background. Never ever scold the dog if they bite. Learn what triggered it and avoid putting them in the position again where biting is seen as their only option. You might have to put up with nips while you learn how to live together.

Coprophagia

This is the behaviour we probably find most disgusting: dogs eating faeces. Many dogs, but especially those from puppy farms, have a tendency to eat either their own or another dog's faeces. As repulsive as it may be to us, there are reasons for this behaviour, especially in the breeding industry survivor. A normal mother will consume the waste from her puppies as she cleans and stimulates them, but it often goes beyond this. Overcrowding, poor quality or lack of food, and aggressive behaviour from a 'cellmate' can also be causes for this. Sometimes, as an act of self-preservation, the dogs may have resorted to this in order to stay alive. Another reason is a simple one: if you can imagine, these dogs have an extremely limited space in which to live, eat, sleep and raise their puppies. They must also defecate in the same area. They are faced with either sleeping in it, or getting rid of it another way.

Once they are rescued, and expected to live in our homes where this behaviour is understandably unacceptable, it can be hard for some dogs to stop doing it as they are so used to consuming it and may actively seek it out. If you have a 'seeker', give them something else to seek. Scatter treats in the garden for them to find before you let them out. They will often turn their attention to finding the treats, especially something particularly delicious like sausage, instead of something nasty. Find what they love and use it. It is not what they are finding that is important, it is the act of seeking that is the distraction. Most importantly, keep the dog's area free of waste. They cannot eat what they cannot find. Do not allow them to go out to the toilet alone. The temptation is going to be greatest right after they have defecated so make sure to be there and distract, clean up or move the dog away from the area.

Regardless of the reason, the cure lies in understanding the unacceptable behaviour, knowing how to intervene and as ever, being patient and not scolding.

The Rewards

These dogs have only known cruelty from humans so they will come round more quickly if there is already a dog in the home, who will show them the way forward to life as it will now be for them: safe, loving and normal.

They do not know how to play and will have no experience of toys. Some can be encouraged to play with toys, others will never understand this. Some will play with resident dogs, often when they think the humans are not watching.

Fear is the overriding emotion that they have ever known. It is the only thing a dog from this background has ever owned in life; it is familiar and in some ways, comforting. It may well be that when an ex-breeding dog has been taken from a puppy farm, for the initial days of freedom he or she would do anything to get back inside the place they have left. It has been all they have ever known. To help them to make the transition from this to the rest of their life, it is helpful to follow these guidelines and be aware of how our actions affect them. Although some may seem a little matter of fact, it will be the quickest way to help them to relax and come round to their new environment. Smothering or pitying them will not help.

Trust is an issue: they have no reason to trust anyone. After years of neglect and abuse, trust must be earned little by little. Be patient. Unfortunately, love and a good heart alone is not enough for these dogs. Understanding their behaviour and how to help them with our own actions is also important.

Adopting an ex-breeder requires more commitment, patience and understanding than adopting a dog who has lived in a home but the rewards are endless. The pleasure of being the one to show an adult dog the world for the first time is priceless. Watching them discover who they are and enjoying treats and comforts for the first time in their lives is rewarding in itself. But the true joy is when that dog first looks at you with love in its eyes – that's pure magic.

But it is important to understand that these dogs will be whatever they decide, not what we decide or want them to be. It is best to have no preconceived expectations of them. We give them a safe, loving home and what they do should then be their choice. They have lived their entire lives being something for other humans – when we adopt them, we owe them not to repeat that. They are not here for us, we are here for them.

If you feel you have got what an ex-breeding dog needs and you are sure that you have both the time and patience to see the process through, give one of these poor souls hope. Help them discover that life does not have to start and end in fear.

Acknowledgements

I didn't know if I would write another book on puppy farming following *Saving Susie-Belle* but thanks to the kind support given to me by friends and so many readers, I am happy that I was persuaded to do so and to share more of Susie-Belle's life and to introduce Twinkle to the world. To every reader I owe great thanks, and even greater gratitude to all who go on to tell others about our story, and the truth that lies behind many of the puppies that are bought today.

Every person that helped me with the first book, and with Susie-Belle, I wholeheartedly thank again, as you are all still here on this journey with us, helping me to keep battling away, and supporting my efforts to do something good in the world. If you weren't around, all of you, it would be a lot tougher to keep fighting to make the misery end for dogs like Twinkle and Susie-Belle.

Much thanks to Marc Abraham for writing the Foreword to this book and for being an inspiration to so many campaigners both in the UK and abroad.

I would also like to give special thanks to Terri Walters, a generous and kind person who gives so much to help all the dogs that she can in her small but amazing rescue. But beyond that, for the generosity of information and guidance given to me in my research, I am deeply grateful. I have been greatly inspired by Mindi Callison – the dedication she shows, standing out in the bitter Iowa cold to protest for the dogs, deserves much recognition, especially as I am often sat tucked up in the warmth of my office when I see her posts on Bailing Out Benji's page. A large ocean stops me being with Mindi and her supporters out on the pavement, but I am always there in spirit.

There are lots of campaigners around the world who I owe much to, many choose to remain quietly behind the scenes and I offer all of you warm acknowledgement, you know who you are. Linda Goodman, founder of C.A.R.I.A.D, Joyce Ireson of Stop Puppy Farming End the Cruelty, and Debra Tranter of Oscar's Law have all been particularly supportive and generous with their time, knowledge and experience. I hope I have done your work justice within these pages.

There have been many that have been happy to share their stories and experiences with me and I hope I have included everything here that you have all wanted shared. Thank you, all of you.

Karen Doonan, co-producer of *Dog By Dog*, began as a useful contact and great source of information, which was always warmly and generously given. And we have a spooky amount in common and are now good friends and I am always going to thank my lucky stars at how they aligned at the right time, allowing us to connect.

Much gratitude to Clare Christian for guidance on publication and valued encouragement. Bev Lawrence for being a trusted sounding board and great supporter of the campaign to end puppy farming.

My deepest thanks go to Michel for letting me disappear for days on end deep in my own thoughts and never seeming to mind, and for his love and unwavering support of everything I do. Finally, I unashamedly thank our girls: Susie-Belle and Twinkle inspire me daily and Renae, for being the perfect sister to them. Without her help, life would not be as much fun for any of us. She makes us smile as we journey together showing her sisters the way and deserves much credit for their happiness.

Further Reading and Resources

I have found the following books fascinating and helpful in developing my understanding of canine lives, the wonder of the unique relationships we share and how I can better improve the world for our dogs:

Bekoff, Marc. *Why Dogs Hump and Bees Get Depressed* (New World Library, 2013).

Bekoff, Marc. *The Emotional Lives of Animals* (New World Library, 2008).

Berns, Gregory. *How Dogs Love Us* (Lake Union Publishing, 2013).

Braitman, Laurel. *Animal Madness* (Simon and Schuster, 2014).

Bradshaw, John. *In Defence of Dogs: Why Dogs Need Our Understanding* (Penguin, 2012).

Grimm, D. *Citizen Canine* (Perseus Books Group, 2014).

Hare, Brian and Woods, Vanessa. *The Genius of Dogs: Discovering the Unique Intelligence of Man's Best Friend* (Oneworld Publications, 2013).

Horowitz, Alexandra. *Inside of a Dog: What Dogs See, Smell and Know* (Simon & Schuster Ltd., 2009).

Kaminski, Juliane and Marshall-Pescini, Sarah. *The Social Dog: Behaviour and Cognition* (Academic Press, Elsevier, 2014).

Moussaieff Masson, Jeffrey. *Dogs Never Lie About Love:*

Moussaieff Masson, Jeffrey. *Why Your Dog Will Always Love You More Than Anyone Else: Reflections on the Emotional World of Dogs* (Vintage, 1998).

–– *The Dog Who Couldn't Stop Loving: How Dogs Have Captured Our Hearts for Thousands of Years* (HarperPaperbacks, 2011).

Oliver, Mary. *Dog Songs* (The Penguin Press, 2013).

White, E.B. Martha White (ed) *On Dogs* (Tilbury House Publishers, 2013).

Organisations and Rescues Located Around the World, Working to Help End the Battery Farming of Puppies and Rehabilitate and Home its Survivors

UNITED KINGDOM

Campaigning Groups

CARIAD CAMPAIGN

PO Box 60

Lampeter

SA48 9BE

http://cariadcampaign.wordpress.com/

A network of charities, organisations, shelters, rescues and campaigns. They undertake investigations and provide evidence for prosecutions, assist with finding homes for the abandoned, unwanted and neglected.

FOUR PAWS

32–36 Loman Street

London

SE1 0EH

http://www.four-paws.org.uk/

International animal welfare charity. Their vision is a world where humans treat animals with respect, empathy and understanding. Their mission is to be the strong, global and independent voice for animals under human control.

NATUREWATCH FOUNDATION
49 Rodney Road
Cheltenham
Gloucestershire
GL50 1HX
http://naturewatch.org/
Naturewatch Foundation is a registered charity working to improve the lives of animals. The Foundation's mission is: to end animal cruelty and advance animal welfare standards around the world. A key part of Naturewatch's work revolves around public education to ensure animals are recognised as sentient beings, capable of suffering, in order to ensure that full regard is always paid to their welfare requirements.

PUP AID
http://www.pupaid.org
Founded by vet Marc Abraham, Pup Aid campaigns to raise awareness and engage people in the political processes that are needed to change the way puppy breeding and sales are regulated in the UK. Pup Aid hosts Europe's largest puppy farming awareness event annually in London.

PUPPY LOVE CAMPAIGNS
http://www.puppylovecampaigns.org
Puppy Love Campaigns carry out undercover investigations to provide evidence of the cruelty of puppy farms in order to educate the public and put pressure on those with the power to close them down.

RSPCA
http://www.rspca.org.uk/home

STOP PUPPY FARMING END CRUELTY (SPEC)
SPEC is dedicated to raising public awareness of the plight of puppy farmed bitches, studs and puppies. They carry out investigations into breaches of licensed premises and

uncovering unlicensed premises, including pet shops.
http://www.stoppuppyfarming.co.uk/

Rehoming Charities
DIANA BRIMBLECOMBE ANIMAL RESCUE CENTRE
Nelsons Lane
Hurst
Wokingham
RG10 0RR
http://www.dbarc.org.uk

EAST MIDLANDS DOG RESCUE
Pingle Farm
Seine Lane
Enderby
Leicestershire
LE19 4PD
http://eastmidlandsdogrescue.org/

FRIENDS OF THE ANIMALS RCT
23 Church Road
Ton Pentre
Rhondda Cynon Taff
CF41 7EB
http://www.friendsoftheanimalsrct.org.uk

HOPE RESCUE
http://www.hoperescue.org.uk

PRO DOGS DIRECT
126 Davenport Road
Catford
London
SE6 2AS
http://www.prodogsdirect.org.uk/

OLDIES CLUB
http://www.oldies.org.uk/

WOOD GREEN, THE ANIMALS CHARITY
King's Bush Farm
London Road
Godmanchester
Cambridgeshire
PE29 2NH
http://www.woodgreen.org.uk/

UNITED STATES

ANIMAL RESCUE CORPS
1380 Monroe St. NW #326
Washington, DC 20010-3452
http://animalrescuecorps.org/
Animal Rescue Corps' mission is to end animal suffering through direct and compassionate action, and to inspire the highest ethical standards of humanity towards animals. They work closely with government institutions, law enforcement agencies, other animal protection organisations and communities to improve and strengthen relationships between humans and animals.

BAILING OUT BENJI
PO Box 203
Ames, Iowa
50010
https://www.facebook.com/BailingOutBenji
A humane education organisation dedicated to raising awareness about animal issues, including puppy mills. Programmes include sending out ambassadors to raise social consciousness about animal welfare issues on a local and national level and holding fundraising events to provide relief to animals in need.

COLORADO CITIZENS FOR CANINE WELFARE (3CW)
PO Box 202713
Denver, CO 80220
http://www.caninewelfare.org/
Colorado Citizens for Canine Welfare's mission is to end puppy mills by educating the public and policy makers about mills and their connection to pet stores, the Internet and other sales venues.

COMPANION ANIMAL PROTECTION SOCIETY
759 CJC Highway, #332
Cohasset, MA 02025
http://www.caps-web.org/
National non-profit organisation dedicated to protecting companion animals from cruelty in pet shops and puppy mills. CAPS actively addresses the abuse and suffering of pet shop and puppy mill dogs through investigations, education, media relations, legislative involvement, puppy mill dog rescues, consumer assistance and pet industry employee relations.

HUMANE SOCIETY OF THE UNITED STATES
PUPPY MILLS CAMPAIGN
http://www.humanesociety.org/puppymills
The HSUS is the nation's largest and most effective animal welfare organisation. Their work is in the US and abroad to protect all animals and to celebrate the human–animal bond, and fight animal cruelty and abuse in all its forms.

SAFEHAVEN SMALL BREED RESCUE
318 Barber Drive
Tionesta, PA 16353
814-463-5004
http://safehavensmallbreedrescue.org/
Based in Pennsylvania, this small, independent rescue does excellent work to rescue, rehabilitate and rehome puppy mill breeders and dogs born in mills with birth defects. There is

a wealth of freely available information on their website to educate the public about the neglect and cruelty that occurs in commercial breeding kennels.

AUSTRALIA

ANIMALS AUSTRALIA
37 O'Connell St
Nth Melbourne, VIC 3051
http://www.animalsaustralia.org/
Animals Australia is Australia's foremost national animal protection organisation, representing 40 member societies and thousands of individual supporters. Animals Australia's vision is a world where all animals are treated with compassion and respect and are free from cruelty.

OSCAR'S LAW
PO Box 4033
Knox City Centre
3152, Victoria
www.oscarslaw.org
Major campaigning group founded by Debra Tranter that campaigns to abolish the factory farming of companion animals, and the sale of factory farmed companion animals from pet shops, online and in print media.

RSPCA AUSTRALIA
http://www.rspca.org.au/

CANADA

ACTIONS SPEAK LOUDER CALGARY (ASLC)
http://www.actionsspeakloudercalgary.ca/
Actions Speak Louder (Calgary) is a volunteer-based campaign concerned with animal welfare and the promotion of knowledgeable and responsible pet guardianship. ASLC discourages finding and purchasing pets online, and promotes the adoption of pets from rescue organisations and reputable breeders.

PEOPLE AGAINST PUPPY MILLS OF ONTARIO
https://www.facebook.com/PeopleAgainstPuppyMillsOntario

THE SOCIAL PETWORK
http://thesocialpetwork.wix.com/thesocialpetwork
A group dedicated to ending the sale of companion animals
in shops.

SOUTH AFRICA

BAN ANIMAL TRADING SOUTH AFRICA
https://www.facebook.com/bananimaltradingsa?fref=nf

For more information about the author and her work follow her on Twitter @SusieBSchnauzer, visit her website www.janettaharvey.com and follow Susie-Belle Schnauzer on Facebook.